Shopping Lists

First published in Great Britain in 2023 by
Cheerio Publishing in association with Profile Books
www.profilebooks.com
www.cheeriopublishing.com
info@cheeriopublishing.com

Photography: Stephen White & Co.
Design: Joe Hales studio

1 3 5 7 9 10 8 6 4 2

Printed and bound in Slovenia by
DZS-Grafik d.o.o.

A CIP catalogue record for this book is available from the British Library.

ISBN 978-1-80081-8132

Ingrid Swenson would like to thank Joe Hales for his superlative design; Clare Conville, Harriet Vyner and Darren Biabowe Barnes at Cheerio and Peter Jones at Profile Books for their encouragement; Steve White and Jackson Pierce White for their photography and friendship; Sally O'Reilly for her enthusiasm and thoughtful comments; Erica Van Horn for her kind support and the extract from The Journal (2007 – ongoing) http://somewordsforlivinglocally.com; and Waitrose. Exceptional thanks go to Andrew Wilson for absolutely everything else. This book is in loving memory of L and K.

FSC www.fsc.org
MIX
Paper from responsible sources
FSC® C106600

Shopping Lists

A Consuming Fascination

CHEERIO

Ingrid Swenson

MINI CHEDDAR

FLAPJACK, x2

SQUEEZE SM

SHREDDIES

YOGHURT + WA

CHICKEN TH

SWEET POTAT

EV/EBITDA

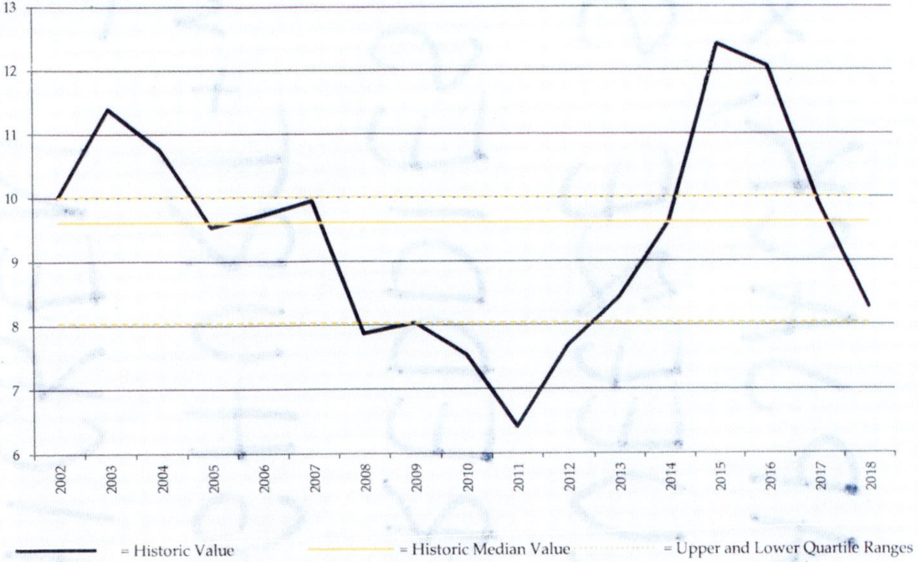

13
12
11
10
9
8
7
6
2002
2003
2004
2005
2006
2007
2008
2009
2010
2011
2012
2013
2014
2015
2016
2017
2018
= Historic Value
= Historic Median Value
= Upper and Lower Quartile Ranges

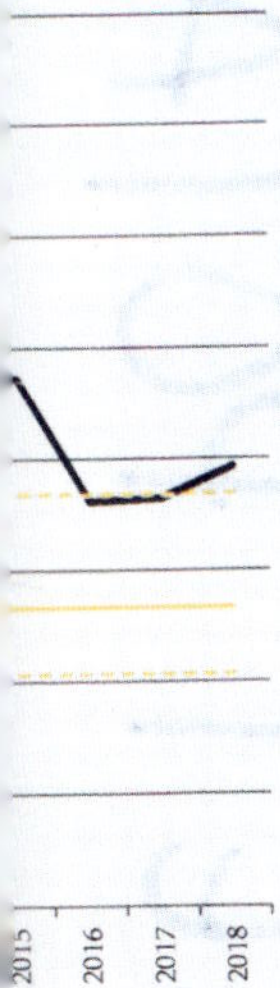

2015
2016
2017
2018

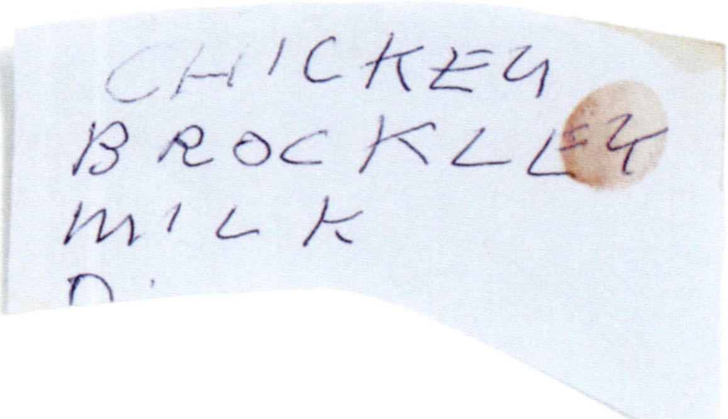
CHICKEN
BROCKLLEN
MILK

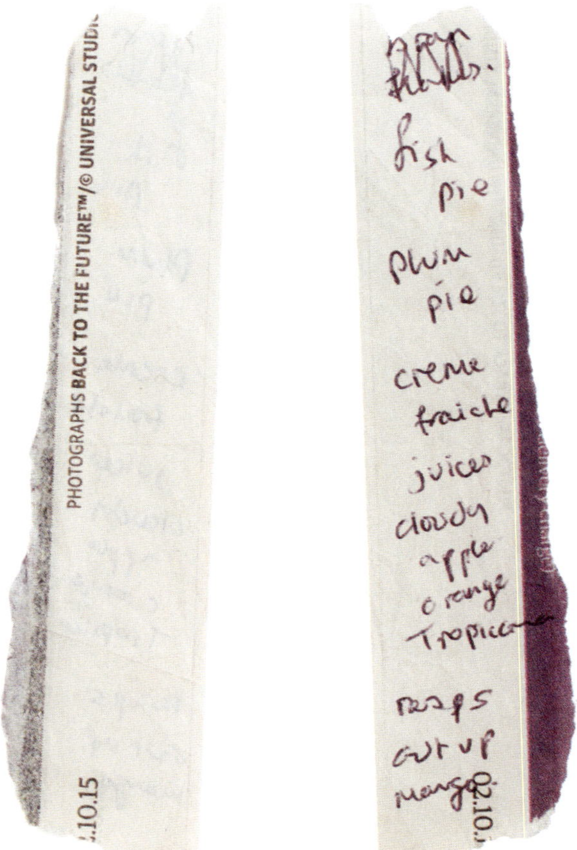
PHOTOGRAPHS BACK TO THE FUTURE™/© UNIVERSAL STUDI
2.10.15
fish pie
plum pie
creme fraiche
juices
cloudy apple
orange
Tropicana
rasps
cut up mango
02.10.

choclat cake
nachr pasta
pasta sauce
milk pizza
Bread juice
Chicken cheese
chicken
nugets
garlic
grapes
Tomatos
ginger

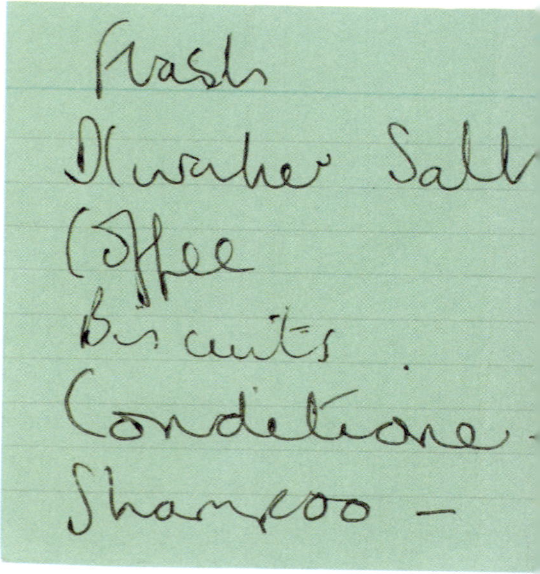
Flash
Dishwasher Salt
Coffee
Biscuits
Conditioner
Shampoo –

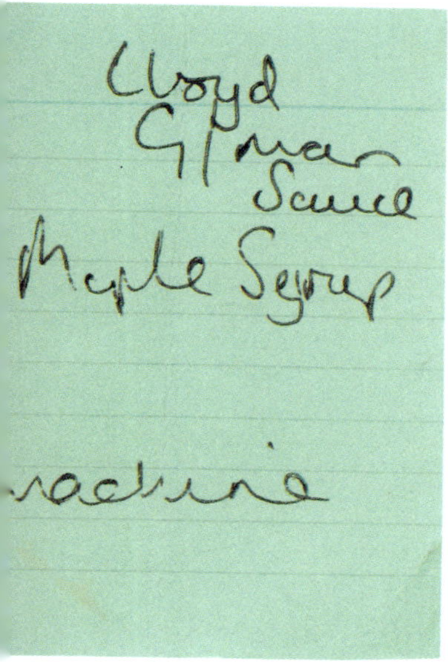
Lloyd
G/man
Sauce
Maple Syrup

machine

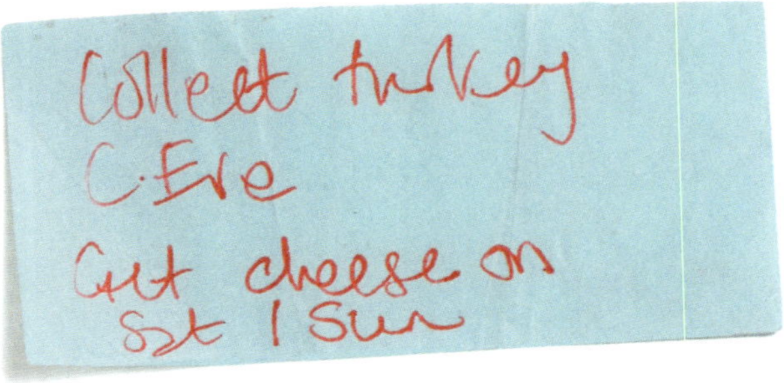
Collect turkey
C.Eve
Get cheese on
Sat / Sun

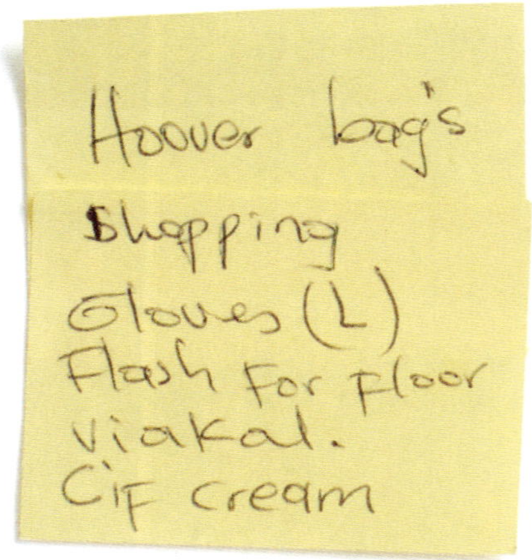
Hoover bag's
Shopping
Gloves (L)
Flash for floor
viakal.
Cif cream

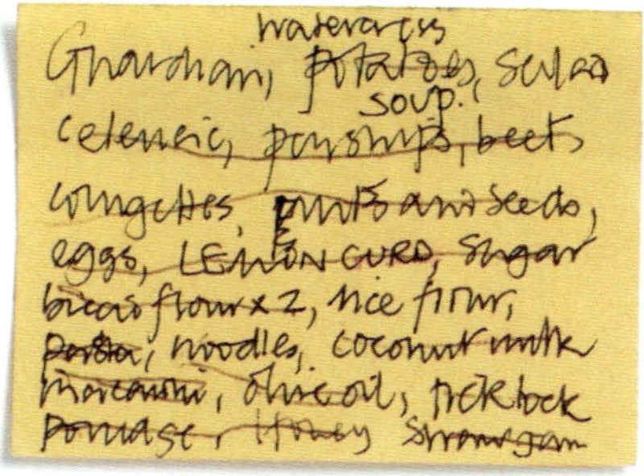
watercress
Guardian, potatoes, salad
soup.
celeriac, parsnips, beets
courgettes, nuts and seeds,
eggs, LEMON CURD, sugar
flour x 2, rice flour,
noodles, coconut milk

THE COLLECTION BEGAN sometime in 2014. I didn't make a conscious decision to start it. I cannot remember the first list I picked up, other than the fact that it contained only a few items. It had been left in a basket and, in one of those clarity-of-vision moments, I instantly thought about the shopping list in a completely new way. It seemed as if someone's entire world had frozen and been captured in a single, modest entity. This thought must have remained with me because I recall that, within a relatively short space of time, I had pocketed a few more lists. I had the sense that I was on to something.

The supermarket was on my cycle route between home and work, so it was a convenient stopping-off point to pick up bits and pieces that could easily fit into my bike paniers. One full shopping basket roughly equated to two full paniers. Mostly carless until my late forties, I've found cycling has been my favourite form of transport since moving to London in the mid 1980s. Even in cold, wet weather, with sufficient layers and waterproofs a bike ride lifts the spirits. These days, I am more often than not overtaken by Lycra-clad whooshes, but the pleasure remains the same. For bulk shops at weekends, I'd drive and enjoy the handy car-parking facility at the rear, uncommon in London for supermarkets so centrally located. Taken together, the weekly supermarket visits by both bike and car could easily number four or five.

In their different ways, cycling, driving and food shopping all provide me with pleasure. My newly acquired hobby of shopping list collecting contributed to and knitted these activities together in a very satisfying way.

Before long, I became a bit more proactive and would purposely hunt them down. This was 'my secret safari', if that is a permissible analogy. It is astonishing how many shopping lists one can find once you start to look in earnest. To the untrained observer, they seem extremely scarce, but once you 'get your eye in' you begin to see them with far greater frequency. On a few occasions I found as many as four or five in one visit. To achieve this could sometimes involve scrabbling about in the ranks of shopping trollies stored both in the car park and large entrance area, or walking unusually slowly through the aisles fixedly focused on the floor. Nobody seemed to notice or care that there was this woman behaving in a strange way. The same few security staff have worked there for years, and I'm sure that one or two of them have cottoned on to what I'm doing, but they have never interfered. The supermarket is a great place to behave oddly in: people just look away.

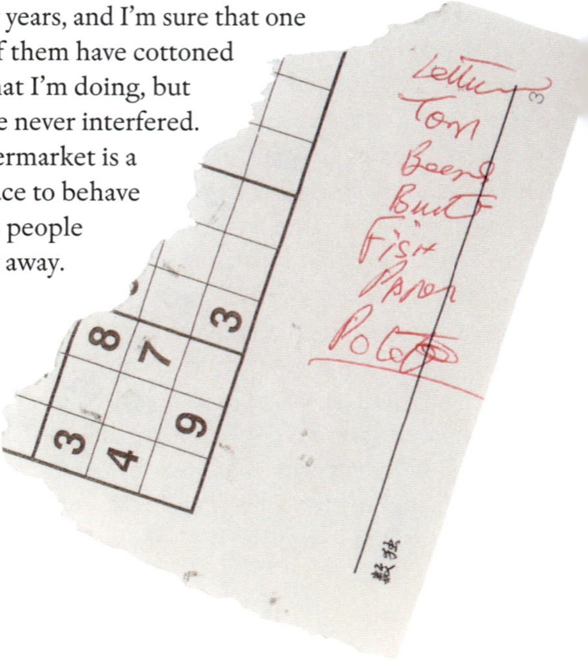

ies
bulter

it's my sodding
my Birthday'
drinks
rinks drinks!

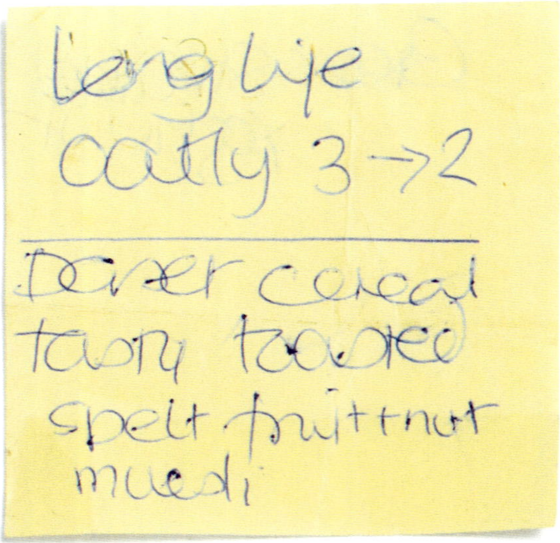
long life
oatly 3 → 2
Dorset cereal
tasty toasted
spelt fruit+nut
muesli

CHOC
Fruit
Yogh
CHOCS
HAM

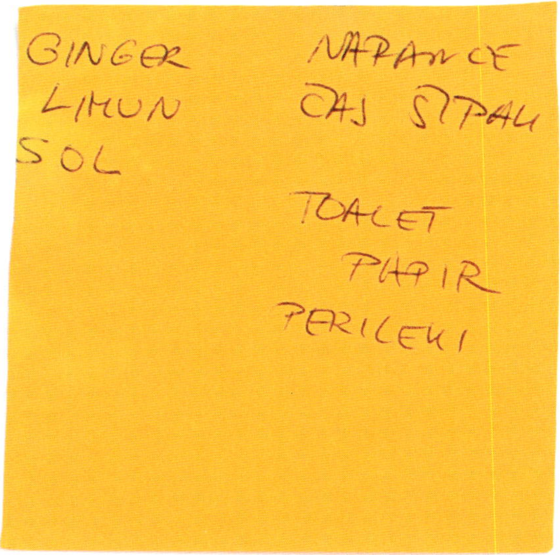
GINGER
LIMUN
SOL
NAPANCE
ČAJ ŠIPAK
TOALET
PAPIR
PERILEKI

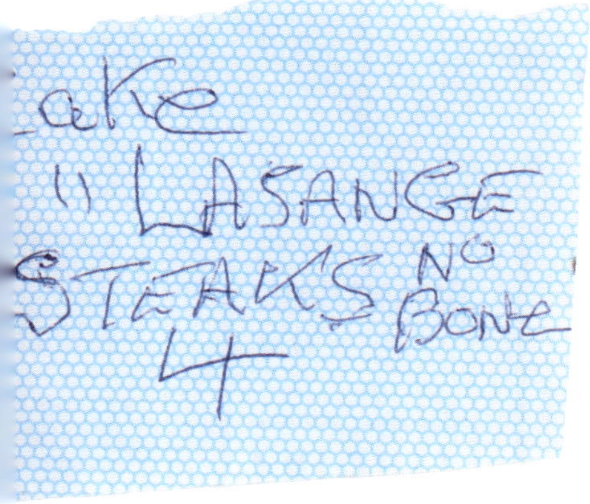
ake
11 LASANGE
STEAKS NO BONE
4

EGGS

AVO

TOMS

BREAD

~~CHEESE~~

G+T

peas
salmon
little gem
bacon
new pots
kitchen roll
prosecco
beers
eggs
washing caps
~~tea~~ napkins
tea
grapes
cheese biscuits
brusshatta bread
rocket
anti bactiral wipes
clothes washing capsules

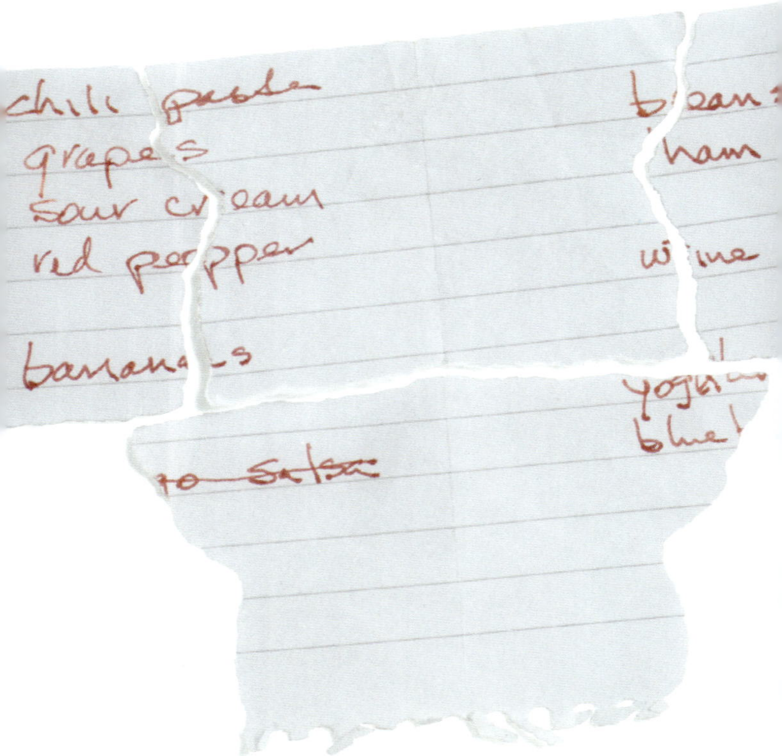
chili paste
grapes
sour cream
red pepper
bananas
ham
wine
salsa

BEERS

Loo roll
Cashew milk
Garlic bread
Lasagna - Pasta sheets
- Mince
- Tomato sauce
- Tomatoes
- Basil
- Carrot
- Cellary
- Sausages
- Milk
- Butter
-

Salad

Potatoes

Cabbage

bog roll

~~Cough medicine~~

Bread

Kim's

fruit

I'M NOT ALONE.

Although I never gave that much thought to whether or not there were other shopping list collectors out there, I've become aware of a small community of us in the last couple of years. Collections in the UK, the US and in Europe have been the subject of books, websites, an exhibition, a weekly newspaper column, even a TED Talk. This has led me to believe that there must be collectors worldwide – in North Korea, Nigeria and New Zealand. Yes, the intrinsic fascination of shopping lists is beguiling and universal. Perhaps an international collectors' club should be formed, and we should start a newsletter. The British branch might be called Potatoes Cabbage Bog Roll.

Although it appears that I'm in good company, I am fairly confident that my collection is unique. My shopping lists have all been collected according to two fundamental, self-imposed rules:

milk

1. They were all found at the Waitrose supermarket on Holloway Road, London N7.
2. They were all found by me.

Occasionally a kindly friend will give or send me a list that they have picked up. One was recently posted from France. Although an excellent list, it was ineligible according to my rules, and therefore has not entered the collection. As far as I am aware, other collections haven't been created according to such stringent rules – contributions from far and wide are actively encouraged, making these collections a far more collaborative or shared activity.

I'm sometimes asked if there is a cataloguing system to record the date found and precise location, whether the lists are organised into any categories, or if I have created an index for analysis purposes, etc. This kind of objective scrutiny has been applied by other collectors, but my lists have not been kept in any particular order. It has never occurred to me to treat them in this way, and it would be challenging and/or excruciatingly boring to do this retrospectively.

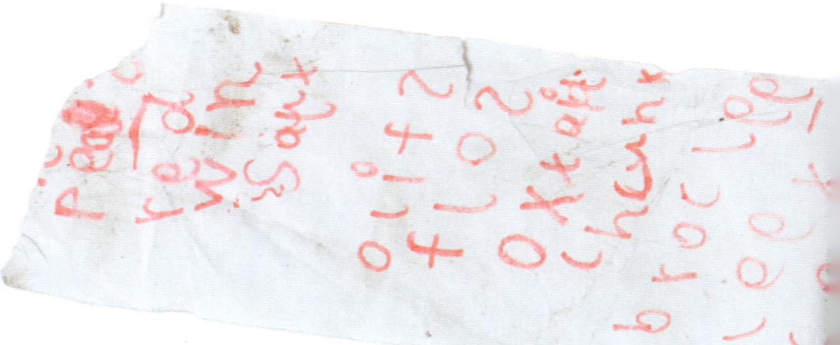

At present, the number of lists I have collected is approaching 1,500.

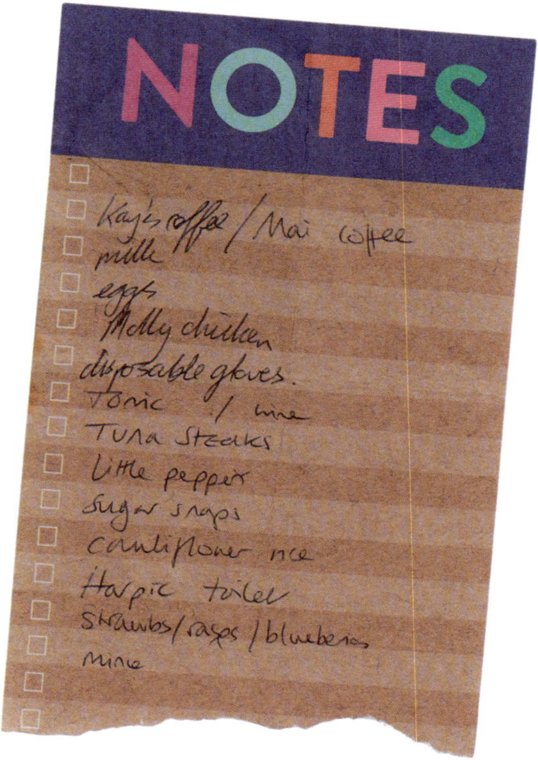
NOTES
Kay's coffee / Mai coffee
milk
eggs
Molly chicken
disposable gloves.
Tonic / wine
TUNA Steaks
Little pepper
Sugar snaps
cauliflower rice
Harpic toilet
strawbs / rasps / blueberries
mince

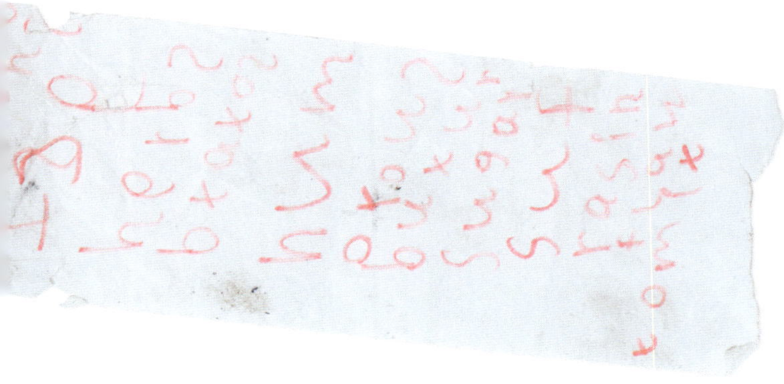

Butter
Flowers
J Rolls.
WATER
FAIRY
PINK
8 ONIONS
milk
Lettuce

Sam
[redacted]

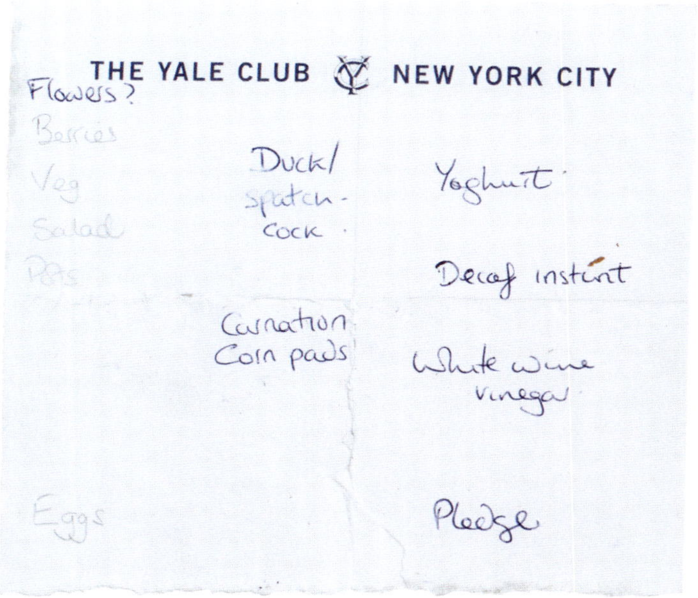

THE YALE CLUB NEW YORK CITY

Flowers?
Berries
Veg
Salad
Pots
Eggs

Duck/
spatch-
cock

Carnation
Corn pads

Yoghurt

Decaf instant

White wine
vinegar

Pledge

Frozen puff
pastry

ubes x 2

3 lge ~~Drinks~~

lge Tomatoes

lge Cold Slaw

1x Cucumber

1x Houmous

Fruit Cocktail

Crisps x 2

4 Yogurts

1x Bread

4x Rolls

lge Couscous

Apricots

Raisins

Dates Figs

Oven dishes

chicken

Vegtable

Roast potatoes

Wedges

Fish

pasta dishes x 2

Chicken dishes x 3

oven dishes

Low fat cheese

Fish Fingers

Fresh Vegetables

Nice Sponge cake

padblocks.com

44 [illegible] nappies milk

nice bread

parmesan

Cheddar

Avocado

hummus

Smoked mackerel

blueberries

courgette

mushrooms

oranges

eggs

bananas

beetroot

pears

organic apples

Dental floss

GOLDFINCH
GREAT SPOTTED WOODPECKER
NUTHATCH
LAPWING
BLUE TIT

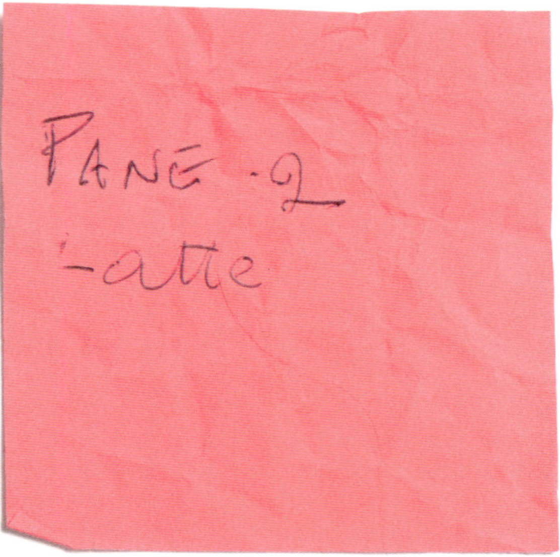
PANE ·2
Latte

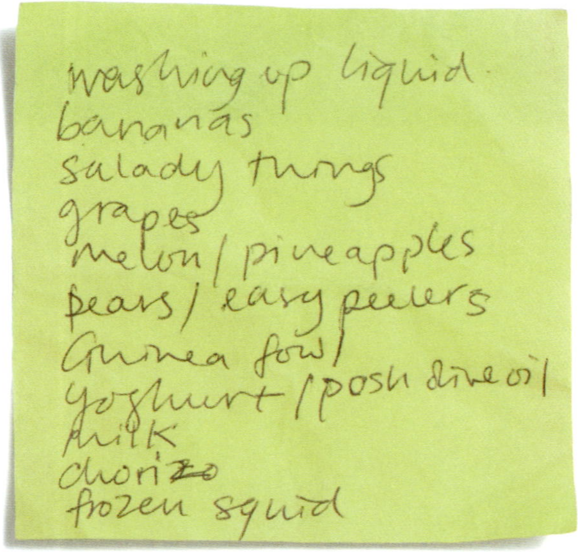
washing up liquid
bananas
salady things
grapes
melon / pineapples
pears / easy peelers
Guinea fowl
yoghurt / posh olive oil
milk
chorizo
frozen squid

wheatabix
Oil
Diabetic choc
 - drink

Salad
onions
tomatoes
- shower gel
- black bags?
-

Oranges, clem
~~[illegible]~~, blueberries
Pots, veg leeks
Humus,
butter, yogh,
Apple juice, muesli
~~Ricecakes~~ -crackers
Meat? Steak

Waitrose shopping list

Guardian	
EW oranges	1.72
EW gala apples	1.00
EW bananas x 5	1.00
2 loose carrots	0.30
EW broccoli	0.37
EW baking potatoes	1.00
baby corn	1.60
Pecans 100g	2.15
piccanti sardines x ~~5~~ 4 + 3 lemon	4.45
EW eggs x 6	1.00
W red curry paste 100g	1.69
Stock cubes 2 pkts	2.50
tin bamboo shoots	0.89
EW tin coconut milk	1.60
Yeo Valley butter x2	3.40
Yeo Valley milk 1 ltr	1.00
EW small chicken	4.39
EW king prawns	2.90
EW toilet rolls x4	1.75
Jackson bread	1.49
W vintage perry	1.90
Pink moscato	6.99
	45.09

icing sugar

W. spinach mornay 1.32

WHILE OTHER SHOPPING list collectors have been keen to dissect and offer interpretations of individual lists by providing their personal analysis, my preference is to show rather than tell. This way we can impose our own readings. Like a private detective, with all of the hard evidence contained in the list, it is possible to build a personal, algorithmic understanding about the shopper.

Items on the list, combined with handwriting and the chosen piece of paper on which to write, are all potential indicators of the shopper's:

age
gender
dietary habits and general health
culture or nationality
proficiency in English
wealth
culinary virtuosity and ambition
if they live alone,
  are in a couple,
  are in a shared house,
  are part of a family with children or teenagers
if there is a special occasion or holiday to be celebrated
their profession – cleaner, poet, actor, student, doctor, literary agent, architect, etc.

~~Basmati 500g~~
~~Rice~~
~~Pasta~~
~~Cous~~
~~100g chapatti flour~~
~~Rose water~~
~~Coriander seeds~~
~~5 cm ginger~~
~~onions~~
~~garlic x2~~
~~1kg lamb shoulder~~
whole milk yoghurt x2
~~saffron~~

~~nappies M~~

~~Coriander x2~~
~~pomegranate~~
~~Lemon~~
~~fresh chilli~~
~~Rapeseed oil~~
~~Mint~~ · ~~Oranges~~
~~basil~~

→ ~~oranges salad~~

~~chips~~ ~~other~~
~~tomatoes~~ ~~onions~~ ~~houmous~~
~~pesto~~ Prosecco?

~~Monkfish~~ / loup + rougets
Haricots verts

Fruits

Bananas
Milk
Cornflakes
Granola
Potatoes
Yogurts
Cheddar
Baked beans
Bread
Falafels
Sour cream
Cucumber
Peppers
Mushrooms
Courgette
Tortillas
Avocado
Aubergines
Onions
Parmesan
Isabelle stock

Sat Fish
Sun –
Mon Fajitas
Tues Aubergine
Wed Artichokes

Parsley
Smoked mackerel
Artichokes

Blue washing machine

Charity shop
Boots – cream
– nappies
– hydrocortisone
– wipes

LIST FOR JOSH FOR GOING TO WAITROSE!

- papaya + fruits.
- Chicken
- avocado
- tomatoes
- potatoes
- juice - lots!
- Shower gel
- pitta
- frijolemole
- hummus
- olive oil
- water
- Kale
- eggs
- Crumpets
- salad
- marmite
- nice yoghurt

58g. Strong cheese
~~Salted~~ butter
Plain flour.

Butter
caster sugar
Plain flour
cheese
salted butter
butter

+ icing ready rolled.

x Sleeping bag.
x M+Spencer Halloween.

anthropologie.com 00800 0026 8476

LONDON • GUILDFORD • BLUEWATER • BATH • LEEDS • EDINBURGH

w/ ~~[crossed out]~~ lobes beef.
Chili puree
Brisket?
Gym
Ham
Campari/milk

Capers
4 tomato
2 cuke
2 red/yellow/green P.
onion red.
Basil.

Veal escalopes 8.
Look what we found *

MK
nectarine
peach
Berry
Plum + ?
(~~[crossed out]~~)

Brie.
Omnivores

2496	14.95
176	13.20
2672	6.75
3.28	
1.49	
1.79	

Crisps (Pombere / Hula Hoops		☐
Sliced wholem bread	coffee	☐
	T bags	☐
Cook apples	Lazy coffee	☐
3 lemons	Wine	☐
6 baby tom,		☐
flat parsley	bin liners	☐
Mint		☐
Cowie	butter	☐
Sp onions	milk	☐
blueberries	Gr Yog.	☐
Spuds.	dairy Yog.	☐
		☐
	bacon	☐
Porridge.	6 Ch breasts	☐
	ham	☐
Dry Lentils 250g		☐
		☐

Ham

Carrots

Brussels Sprouts

Broccolli

Potatoes

Tinned Tomatoes

Salad

White cabbage

Carrots

Garlic

Tomatoes

Lettuce

Chipolatas }

Bacon }

Stuffing

Chicken

Olive Oil

Cat Meat

Toilet Paper

Bread /Bagels

Milk

Fruit Juice

Honey

Cheese

Maple Syrup

Fizzy H_2O

Vit C.

Potatoes

nappies.

Yoghurt

Salmon

bolognaise veg

joint

Rolls
Garlic
Tuna
Bread ?
Berries

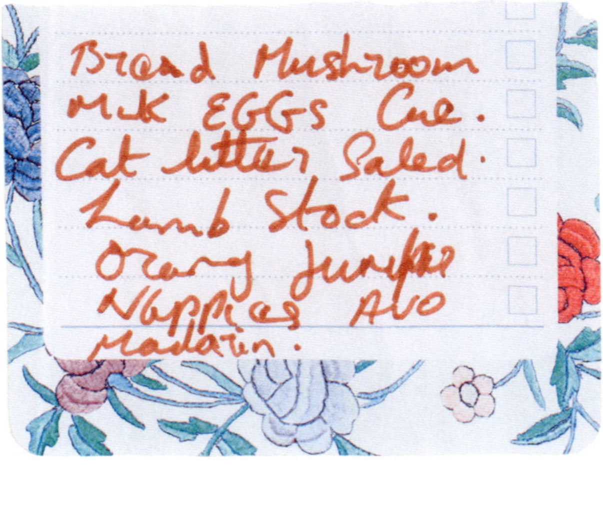
Bread Mushroom
Milk EGGs Cuc.
Cat litter Salad.
Lamb Stock.
Orange Juice
Nappies Avo
Madarin.

~~Hand wash~~

~~T.V. Prop~~

~~Lemons~~

~~Veg.~~

~~Fruit~~?

Tonic

Cordial

Milk

Lights

Meat?

~~Toms~~

Pastry

~~Mushrooms~~

366 Holloway Rd

~~Friday~~ Transport

10.30 - 12.30 P.M

AM

Butter

Banana

Porrage.

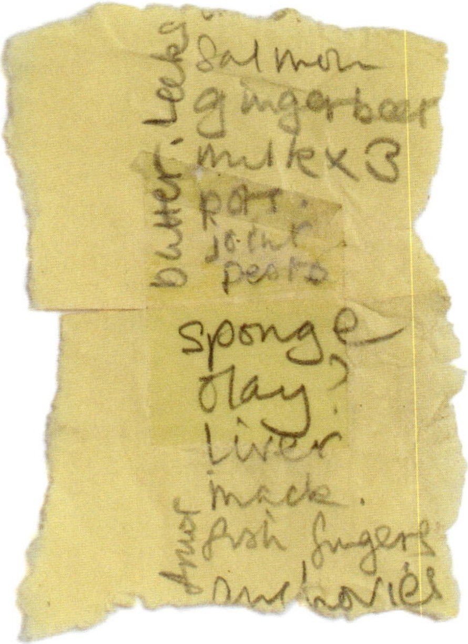
Salmon
gingerbeer
milk x 3
port
joint
pesto
sponge
Olay?
Liver
mack.
fish fingers
butter.
Leeks

IN THE FIRST couple of years of collecting, the trolleys had little upright clipboards attached to the centre of the push bars, handily designed for shoppers to clip their lists onto. These were an extremely rich source of list-finding, but it was a bit like shooting fish in a barrel. These finds gave me nowhere near the same sense of satisfaction as the detection of a good list on a tiny crumpled-up piece of paper on the floor, or spotting one that had been trampled into pitted wet tarmac and peeling it off gently so as not to tear the fragile soaking paper. These early, easy clipboard pickings didn't last long. To stem the scourge of trollies being borrowed, the chain-attachable coin-slot trolley was introduced, and in order for them to nestle neatly in ranks, and for the shopper to be able to retrieve their coin, the clipboards had to be removed.

I imagine that there had been serious discussions at management level before taking this action. Waitrose rightly prides itself on excellent customer service and, aside from the palaver of having to scrabble about looking for a pound coin, the inconvenience of having the handy clipboard removed must have disappointed many shoppers. Tokens branded 'Waitrose' were for a time distributed freely to loyal shoppers to alleviate the former problem, but these soon ran out.

The number of lists found each week did fall at around the same time that the clipboard-less trollies were introduced. But my sense was that this decline also corresponded with the increased use of the notebook function on mobile phones, as well as the growth of online billing – and consequently the significant reduction of used envelopes available to write lists on. By the time of the first lockdown – and four years after

Air Freshener
Holly
COAL
Pens club.

walnuts
cashews

the start of the collection – shopping habits were already changing. The impact of the pandemic meant that spontaneous IRL shopping was actively discouraged and with it, too, the shopping list. As life becomes more digital, more efficient and more ecologically aware, the shopping list, as a quotidian fact of life, like so many everyday items, sounds and smells, is gradually dying out.

~~Coffee~~

~~Washing up l.q.~~

Salt

~~[illegible]~~

~~[illegible]~~

~~[illegible]~~

~~Chicken~~

~~Peppers~~

~~[illegible]~~

~~Onions~~

~~[illegible]~~

~~Chorizo~~

~~Prawns~~

~~Carrots for Dad.~~

GIN

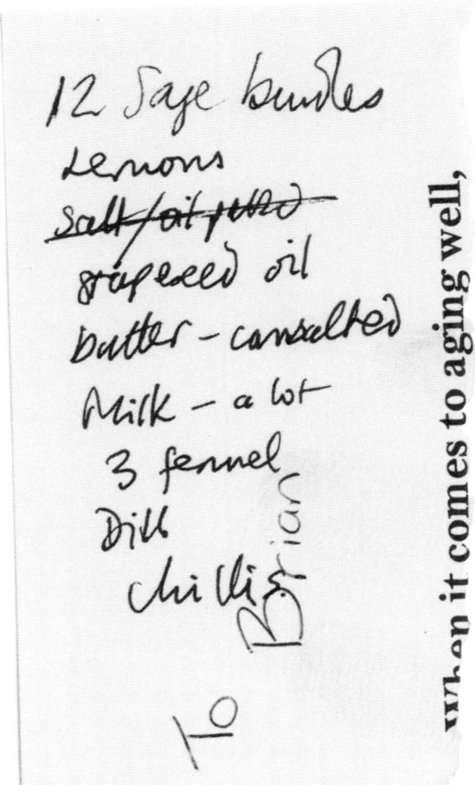
12 Sage bundles
Lemons
~~Salt/oil pesto~~
grapeseed oil
butter – unsalted
Milk – a lot
3 fennel
Dill
Chillis
To Brian
when it comes to aging well,

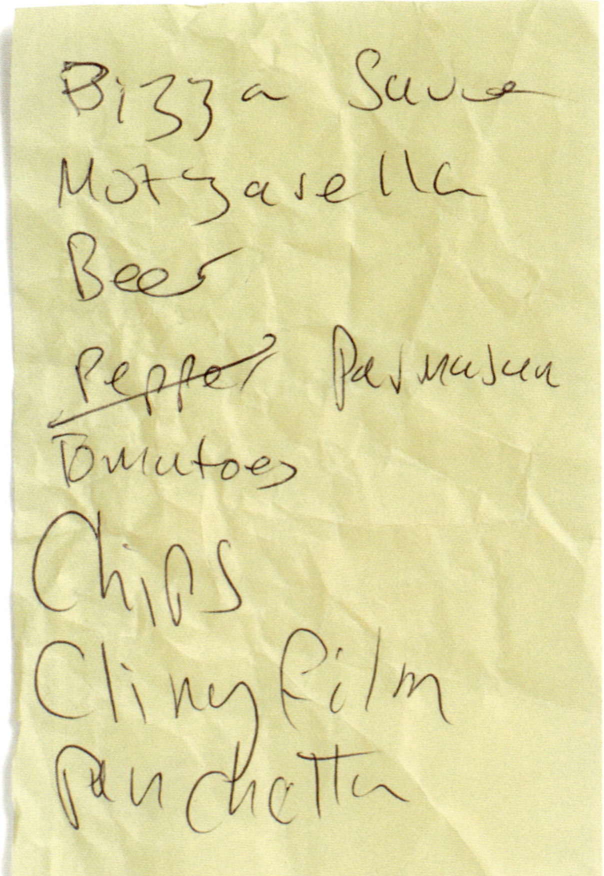
Pizza Sauce
Mozzarella
Beer
~~Pepper~~ Parmesan
Tomatoes
Chips
Cling film
Pancetta

POT GREEN LEEK TOM
CARR

BREAD

PUREE

MILK FLORA

Chilli oil

peppercorns

washing up liquid

~~[illegible]~~ coffee

tissues

mayo

cereal x3

CEASAR SALAD
TOMS.
LEMON.
BUTTER
CREAM
CHEESE/SLIC.
FRUIT/SEAN
FROZE FRUIT
YOGART

Κρεμίδια
ντομάτες
Πατάτες
φιστικέλαιο
χάρτι λουκουμια
Λουκουμια
Μήλα
Αυγά

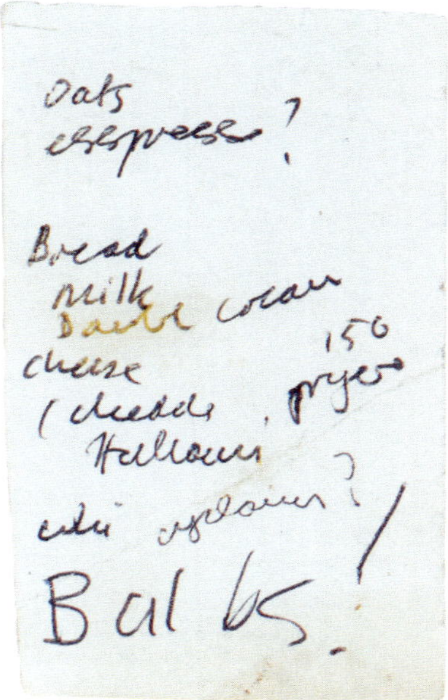
Oats
?
Bread
milk
cheese
150
Halloumi

IDL

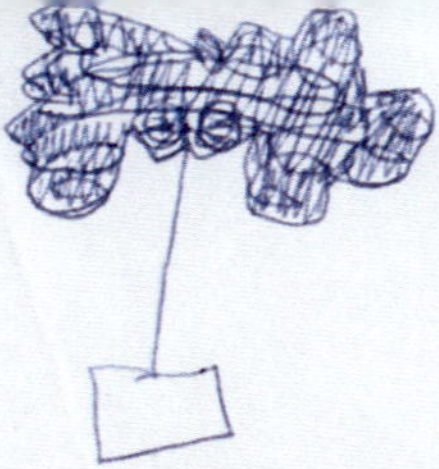

- Lemons 
- ~~Bread~~ 
- ~~Fish?~~  /Fish Pie 

~~Apples~~ 

~~Ham~~ 
PARMA

Dog 

Busta con verdure x minestrone

THE ACTIVITY OF shopping list collecting has elements of scavenging and foraging, and I consider myself to be adept at both. The former being an opportunistic activity and the latter a more benign and wholesome pursuit.

Scavenging is usually thought of as an urban occupation and associated with picking up or consuming debris from our material culture. Wildlife migration to metropolitan areas is primarily due to scavenging opportunities. Pigeons, rats and, more recently, foxes are good examples of fauna that thrives better in cities. Scavenging tends to be used pejoratively, for both animals and people, but is an effective way of recycling, which of course is otherwise encouraged. I enjoy looking into skips, and gratefully bring home things that people have wilfully, or not, deposited on the street for the taking. Recent examples include lamps, books, an enamel roasting tin, nearly dead houseplants, a jigsaw puzzle, a child's school chair.

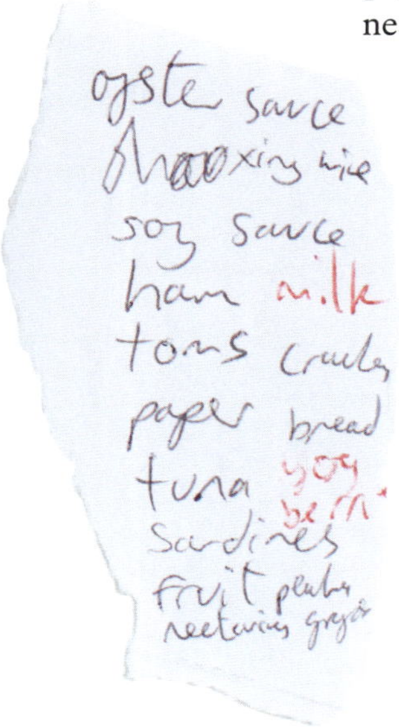
oyste sauce
soy sauce
ham milk
toms
paper bread
tuna
sardines
fruit

Foraging is traditionally thought of as a countryside occupation as a way of benefiting from and reaping the rewards of nature's bounty. The correlation between being in nature and happiness is well known and documented. Unlike the uninvited scavenger, whose actions are generally discouraged and considered unwholesome, the activity of foraging is regarded

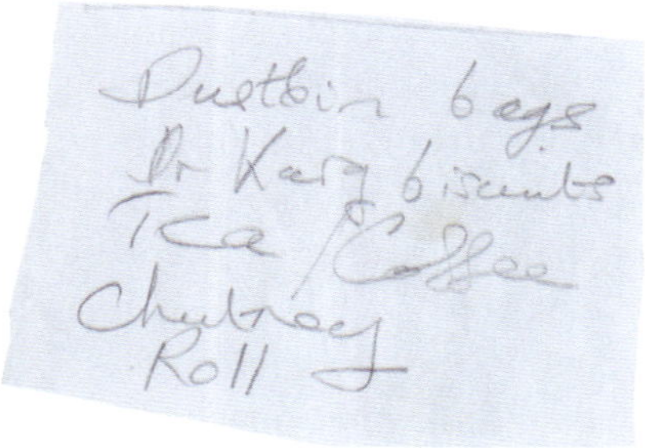
Dustbin bags
Dr Karg biscuits
Tea / Coffee
Chutney
Roll

as a healthy and positive one. In recent years – especially for people with limited access to nature – city foraging has become very popular, in parks, open spaces, cemeteries and at the easily accessed edges of urbanisation. The wellbeing properties of foraging also have business potential. Corporate team-building exercises and staff away-days themed around collective foraging outings are easily secured online, and individual places for the monthly 'Wild Food and Nature Walks' in London are offered for £50 a head.

Although my conduct when collecting shopping lists is perhaps more akin to that of a scavenger, the positive impact that this activity has had for me is closer to that of the forager.

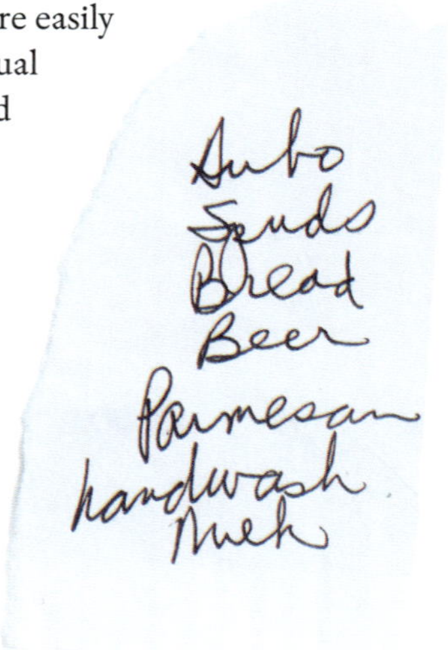
Bread
Beer
Parmesan
handwash

parsley
halouni
parmesan
cans
tomatoes
onions
soappowder.

TREACLE
PRAWNS
C. cheese.
Tin Toms
Soup
Salmon.
KIWIS

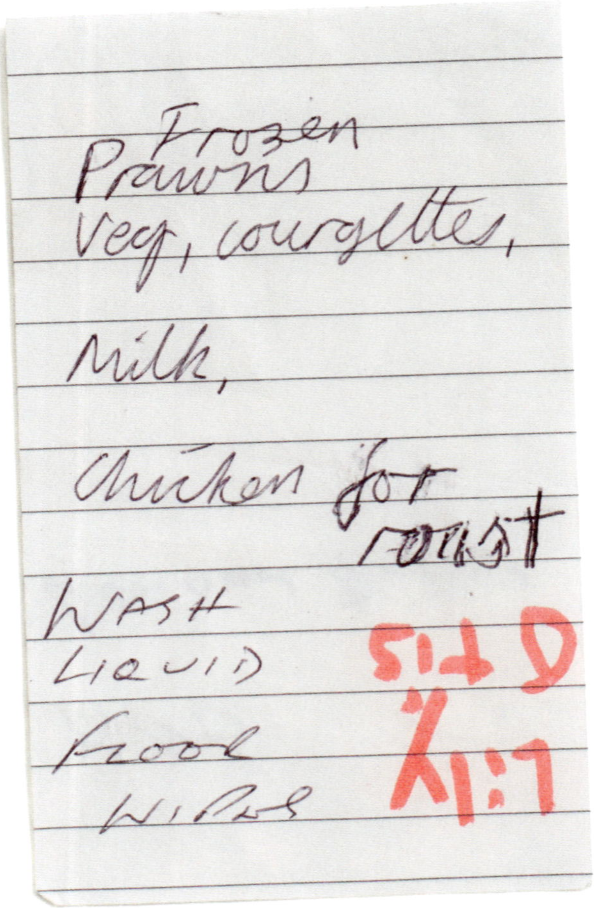
Frozen
Prawns
Veg, courgettes,
Milk,
Chicken for
roast
WASH
LIQUID
Flood
Wipes
Lily
Otis

HI CAZ,

please may you get me:

- punnet of green grapes
- spinach
- peppermint tea
- frozen blueberries if they have them
- toilet roll
- Bananas X 2

Thanks

xBxBxB

Caster sugar
Baking powder
Soy sauce
Sesame oil
bin bags
AA batteries
Dishwasher cleaner

- fruit
- jams
- steak.
- icecream.
- milk.
- rice.
- salmon.
- bread.
- parsley
-

- celery X2.
- almond milk.
- passata.
- halloumi

Porridge
Frutta
Patate
Ham.
Veg.

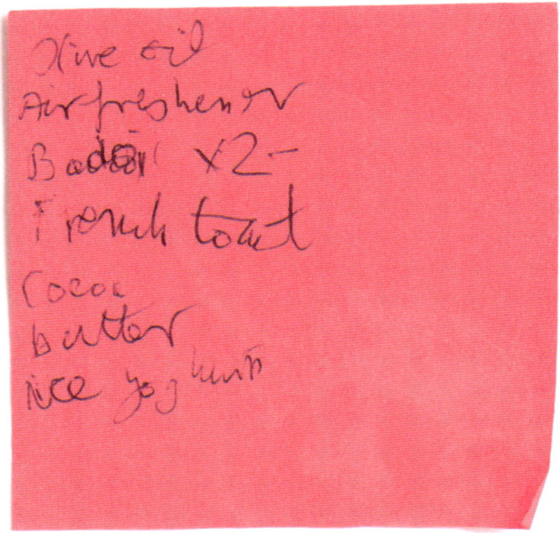
Olive oil
Air freshener
Bacon x2 -
French toast
Cocoa
butter
ice yoghurt

Raisins

Orange Juice

Bananas

Meuseli

~~Bagatte~~

Tissues -

Box Tissues

Fish.

Blue Milk

Cheddar Cheese

Big Potatoes.

- - - - - - - -

Chicken

Ham

Eggs.

Carrots

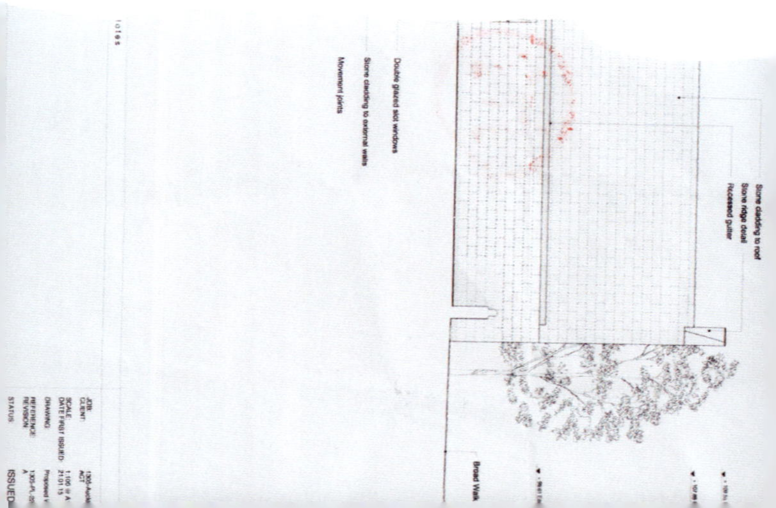
Double glazed slot windows
Stone cladding to external walls
Movement joints
Stone cladding to roof
Stone ridge detail
Recessed gutter
Broad Walk
JOB:
CLIENT:
SCALE:
DATE FIRST ISSUED:
DRAWING:
REFERENCE:
REVISION:
STATUS:
ISSUED

Bacon
Wine
Chicken stock
Chicken
Tarte citron
Raspberries
Creme'

3 f lemon
Nutella

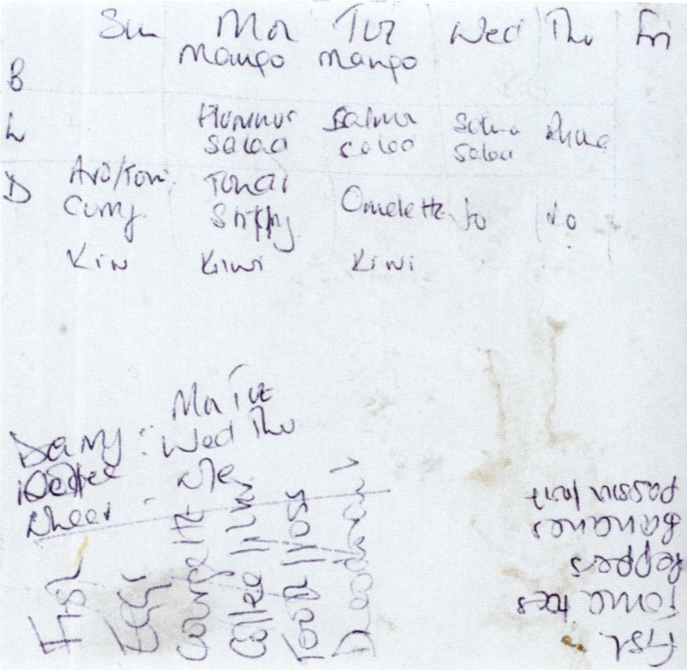

Sun
Mon
Tue
Wed
Thu
Fri
B
mango
mango
L
salad
salad
salad
D
Curry
Omelette
Kiwi
Kiwi
Wed Thu
Dairy
Eggs
Fish
tomatoes
peppers
bananas

1. Self raising flour
light & fluffy

2. Large eggs

3. black currant
jam

4. cream (whipping)

5. butter or Stork

6 table clothe

7. bread

~~8. Lemons~~ Lemons

9. soup

10 Tea bags

11. plastic bags

12 wetex

13. Lunch for Adrian

Loo paper

E.L.

kleenex

Blues / Strawbs,
Lemons

Sm Potatoes
& ~~B~~ Carrots
Cauli.fl /
Celery fennel
Mushrooms
Etc.

Ham x 4
ve regul

Alm M x 3

Sm Udo x2

Bread

Eggs x 2

Times

OWED £8.00
10/3/16

~~[illegible]~~

Bircher Muesli

~~[illegible]~~

Tea (black + fruit)

Frozen fruit.

Lentils (red)

Veg.

Chicken

Sweet potatoes

Almonds.

Asparagus

Chillis

wine in Whitstable

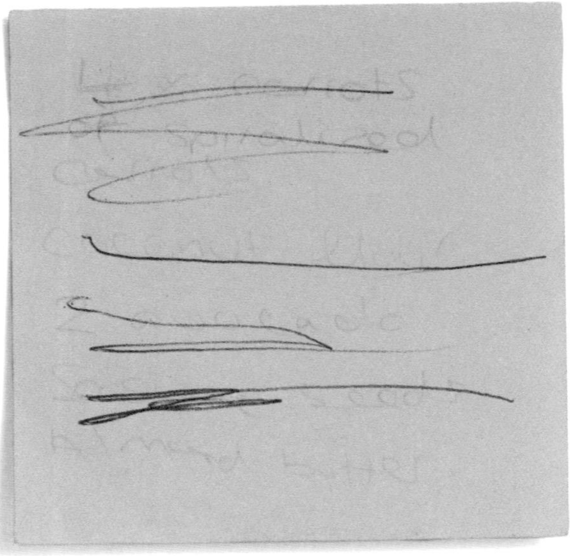

bread
1 onion
250g button mushrooms
400ml reduced fat coconut milk

Shoping list

so much to do
so little time

shopping list
SHOPPING

PLANTS
~~KITCHEN T~~
~~SHAMPOO & CON.~~
~~DUSTBIN.~~
~~EAR B BUDS.~~
~~COTTON PADS.~~
~~SEADS.~~
~~WATERING CAN.~~
plant for are man
table cloth PVC
Drain unbloker
New bath plug
fake flowers

to do

Strawberrys

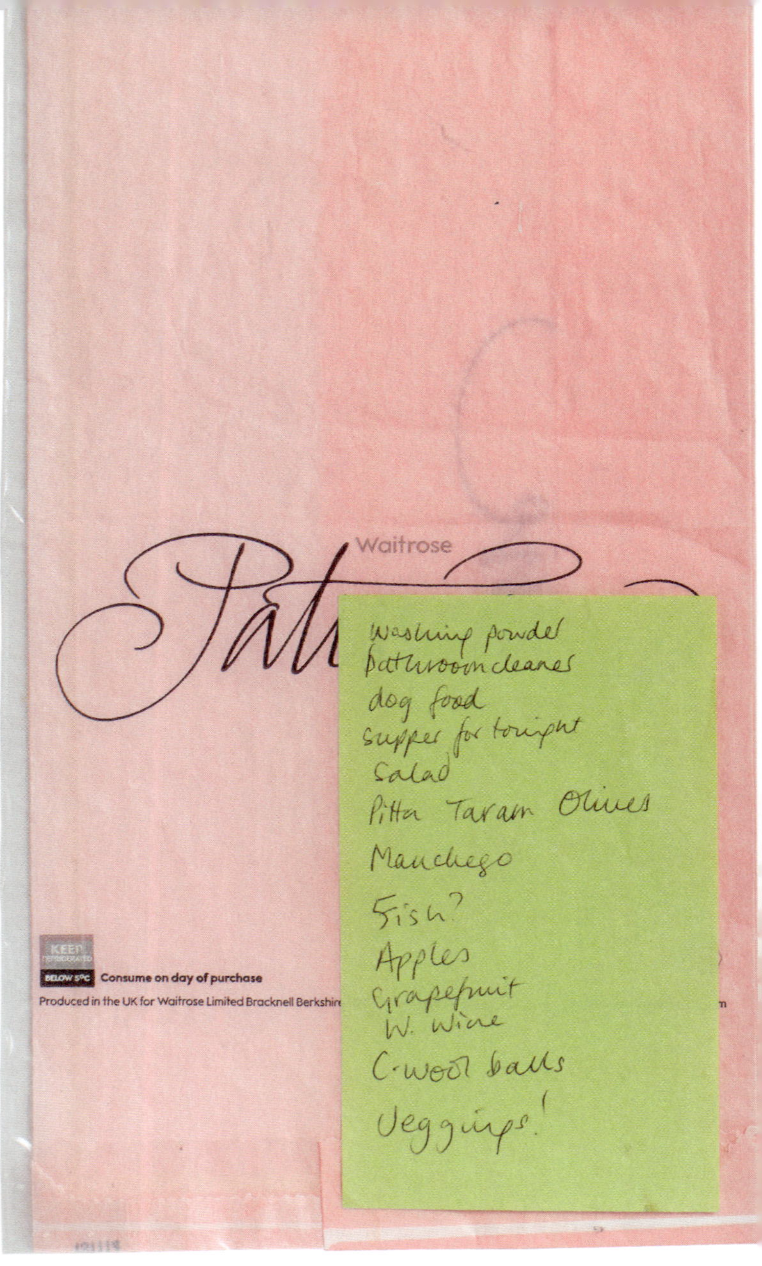
Waitrose
KEEP REFRIGERATED
BELOW 5°C
Consume on day of purchase
Produced in the UK for Waitrose Limited Bracknell Berkshire
washing powder
bathroom cleaner
dog food
supper for tonight
Salad
Pitta Taram Olives
Manchego
Fish?
Apples
Grapefruit
W. Wine
C-wool balls
Veggings!

5475

PRAWNS.

TURKEY SLICES

490=80 x 3

1472=90

4794=74

NUTS

PANCETTA

BANANAS
APPLES
CHIVES

EMERGENCEE

EGGS

FALAFEL

YOGHURT

BAKED BEANS

SAUSAGES

PRAWNS

MANGO

SEEDED FISH

PINE NUTS

MAPLE SYRUP

MILK

APPLE PIE BARS
MAPLE CORN FLAKES

[illegible]
BROWN
SUGAR

NUTS

Bananas
apples.
~~broccoli~~
Smoothie tubes (innocent).
frubes or equivalent. (whi
Bread
2 pints milk
peanut butter
Juice 3 fr £4 - orange j
caster sugar.
goodies fruitbars 2 fr £4.

er is cheaper).

, orange & mango, apple juice

Soup
toothpaste
Liver
green pepper
g-f muesli

Priscilla
milk

oregano

Moose
bread
pastries
Chicken

Vodka +
fags

½ CHICK
2 STEAKS
HAM
Celery
CAKE

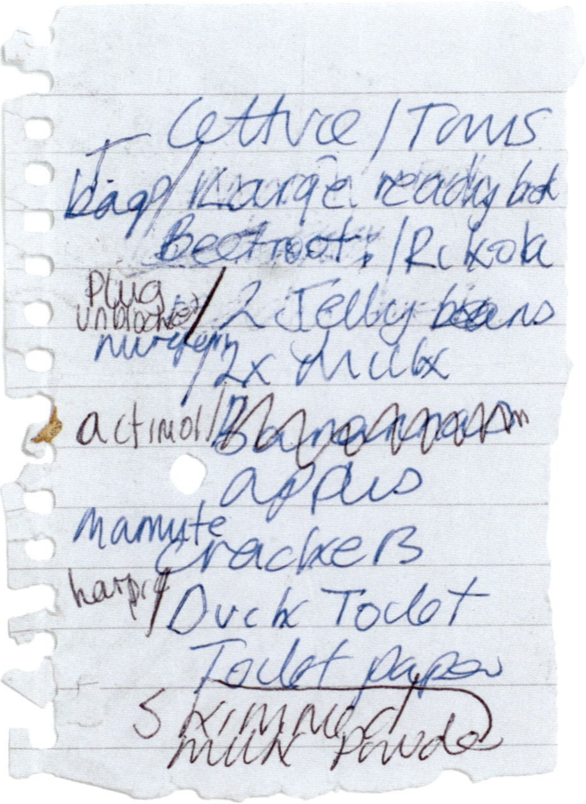
Lettuce / Toms
bagg Marge. ready bck
Beetroot / Ricotta
Plug unblocker / 2 Jelly beans
nurofen / 2x milk
actimol / Bananas
apples
Marmite crackers
hairpig / Duck Toilet
Toilet paper
Skimmed milk powder

~~Food / Presents~~

~~Baby Bread~~

~~crackers~~ / Beetroot

3+2 lettuce / Toms

1 apples / Milk

toilet paper

~~mouthwash~~

Sanitary towels

hand cream / ~~nurofen~~

bin bags

Flash bath / Large Sponges

- gnocchi 800g
- eggs.
- 250 asparagus

- passata.
- Butter beans.
- feta 100g
- loo paper
- Toothpaste
- Flour.
- plums.

THE POSITIVE/NEGATIVE connotations associated with the activities of scavenging/foraging is echoed in the nuanced ambiguity of the lists themselves. Are they trash or treasure? Somewhere in between, or both? Their categorisation and status as litter is perhaps a misnomer altogether. I doubt that the majority of people who drop their lists or leave them in a shopping trolley would also happily toss a crisp packet or sweet wrapper on the ground.

The lists have mostly been abandoned or lost, not maliciously littered. Simply left behind, wholly beyond use and forgotten about. I've often checked the rubbish bins for them, thinking that people would dispose of them 'responsibly', but it is surprisingly rare to find lists that have been thrown away intentionally.

Personally, I am not aware of ever having lost a shopping list. Left at home, frequently, but not lost while shopping. It would seem that the vast majority of lists arrive and leave the supermarket with the shopper who will, like me, regularly find expended lists in a pocket or bag before disposing of them at home.

The possibility remains, however, that perhaps some shoppers may have left their lists intentionally to be seen by others. Perhaps they are meant to be found and read as a way of marking territory, and to share with the world their gastronomic preferences? It is possible to identify several examples of lists as being by the same hand – shoppers who repeatedly abandon, drop or misplace their list. In these cases, the items on the lists as well as the physical size and type of paper used also tend to be very consistent. One shopper in particular leaves their lists behind with such frequency – aways in the trolley, always on the same, multiple note cards and always in the same large, cursive, stylish, self-confident script – that one can only assume that these are a deliberate form of communication. Their author is saying, ‘Look at my world of wonderful food that I love to eat.’

potatos
for
mashing

please
prepare
mash to
go on top
of shepherds
pie

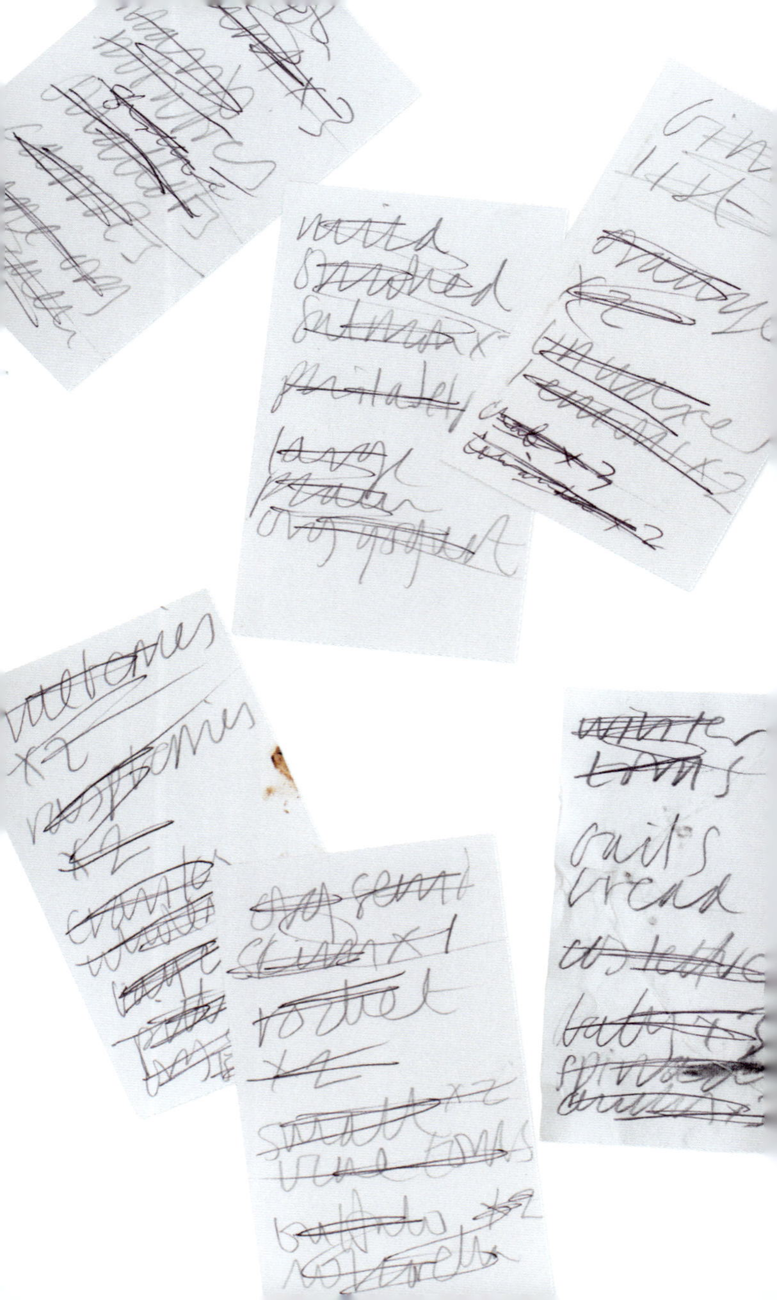

almonds
x2
mint
parsley
basil
milk x1
thursday
dried
apricots
x2

please prepare escalopes
dry clean
mustard
cloves
peppercorns

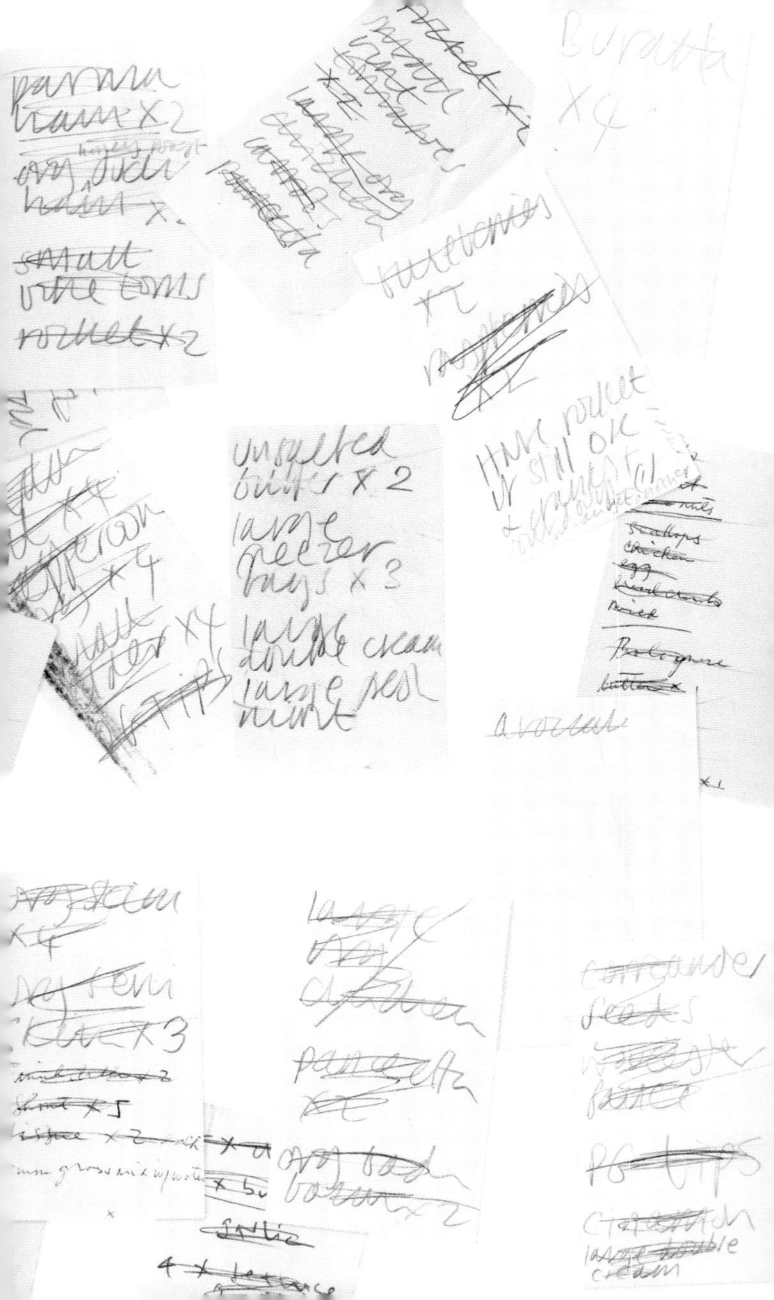
parma ham x 2
Burrata x 4
unsalted butter x 2
large freezer bags x 3
large double cream
Scallops
Chicken
egg
Bolognese
coriander seeds
large double cream

paper Ro
Cling Fi
Star a
anchovi
capers.
Cinnamo

1 bleach
1 Viakal
1 Cif POWER Bathroom
1 Duck (Toilet)
1 Glass cleaner
1 Floor Clener
1 Cif Cream
1. fuerniture polish.

poetry london

Thank you for sending your work to *Poetry London*. We are sorry we cannot offer you publication. We regret too that, because of the volume of submissions we receive, it isn't possible to give an individual response.

Your interest in the magazine is greatly appreciated, and we wish you every success with your writing.

Your submission has been considered by Martha Kapos, who is editing the Summer issue.

Martha Kapos, *Assistant Poetry Editor*
Ahren Warner, *Poetry Editor*

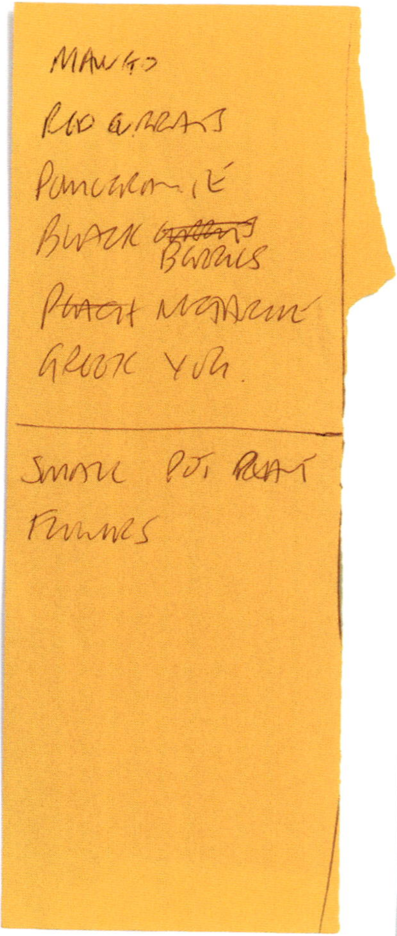
MANGO
RED CURRANTS
POMEGRANATE
BLACK BERRIES
PEACH NECTARINE
GREEK YOG.
SMALL POT PLANT
FLOWERS

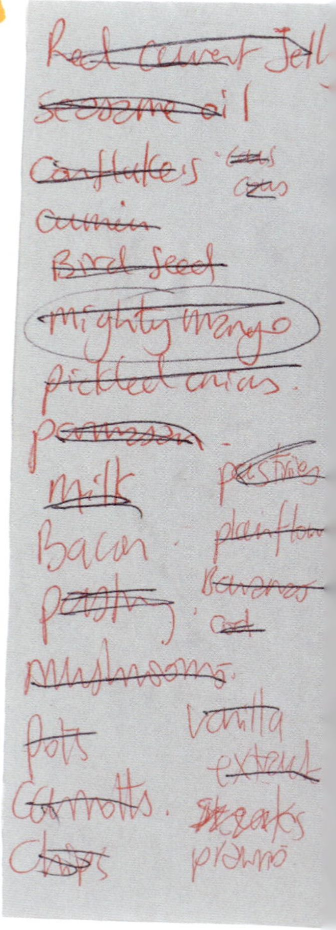
Red currant Jelly
Sesame oil
Cornflakes
cumin
Bird seed
mighty mango
pickled onions.
parmesan
milk
pastries
Bacon
plain flour
Bananas
pastry
cod
mushrooms.
Pots
vanilla extract
Carrotts.
steaks
Chips
prawns

• Lge full cream organic MILK

Melon + Strawberrys

Salad. • 1 Lge tomatoe.

Lime

tea bags

granola x 2. – rude Health 'The granola' + Dorset cereals 'chocolate granola'

Dish cloths

Lighters x 2

Cin Sticks

Bog Roll – white

Spaghetti. • Sour cream

• Tortilla chips

poo Bags. • Juice – cordial

Mayo.

500 minced beef

R. pepper

x 2 tins of tomatoes + Tin of kidney beans

fresh coriander

cheese
eggs
min
coffee
milk
fruit
yog
beer
tonic
white persil
crackers
toms.
Bread wh + br sliced
fish fingers
ham
UHT milk
Cream
Veg

desserts
fruit juice
beer
toothpaste.
potatoe
fish mix
mushrooms.
butter block
gin
biscuits
whisky

guardia

an Weekly
Way, Ashby Park, Ashby-De

enicillin

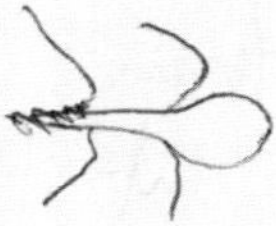

s:

number: + 44 (0) 330 333 67
ress: gwsubs@theguardian.cc

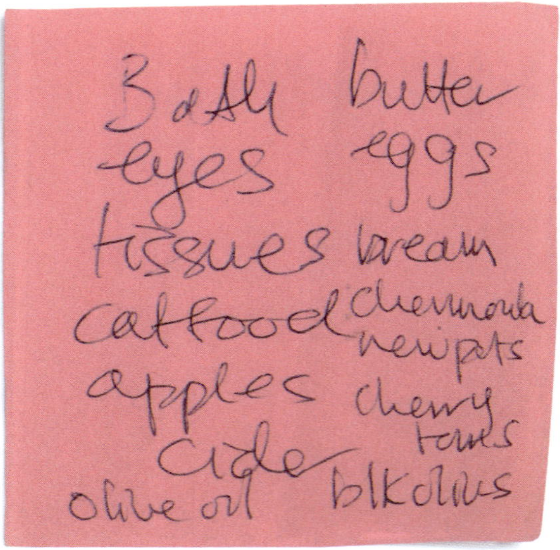
3 Bath
butter
eyes
eggs
tissues
bream
catfood
chermoula
newpots
apples
cherry
toms
cider
blk olives
olive oil

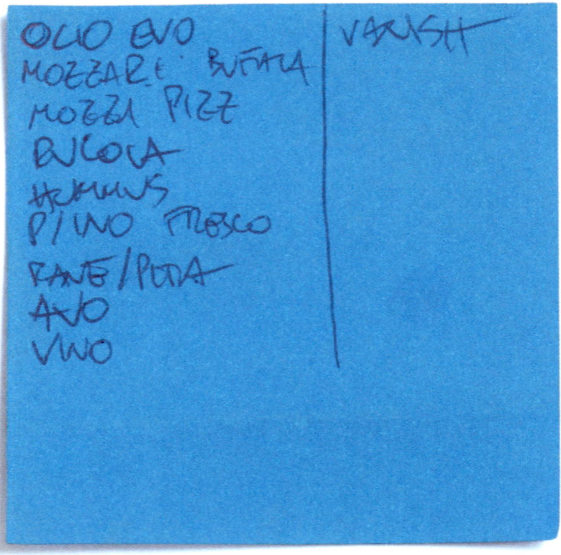
OLIO EVO
MOZZARE BUFALA
MOZZA PIZZ
RUCOLA
HUMMUS
PINO FRESCO
PANE/PITA
AVO
VINO
VANISH

oranges
kitchen Roll
Brillo

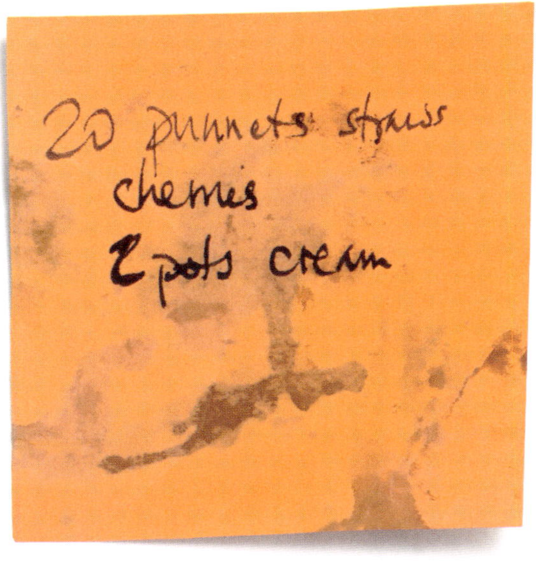
20 punnets straws
cherries
2 pots cream

Ingredients
for chicken stir fry
(noodles, beansprouts etc.)
sauce
Rik cliks + tins
OJ + Apple J.
biscuits.
thin choc.
straws + } voucher
Sun. meal.
eggs bacon saus.
dishwash liq.
wine
Vanish white.

37 INT. LYELL CENTRE, HARRY AND NIKKI'S OFFICE - NIGHT 2 - 20:02 37

NIKKI sits at her desk.

ZAK (O.S.)
Night, Nikki.

NIKKI looks across to ZAK leaving. Throws him a smile.

NIKKI
Night...

ZAK exits and NIKKI quickly gets to her feet...

CUT TO:

38 INT. LYELL CENTRE, COLD STORE - NIGHT 2 - 20:03 38

NIKKI enters the cold store. LEO has removed the BOG GIRL from the mortuary fridge. Spray in hand, he's examining the outside of her RIGHT THIGH, whilst the Bog Girl's LEFT THIGH remains immersed in peat.

NIKKI
Leo?

Eggs ½ doz (will get more @ cherry Gardens)
beer

broccoli
onions
little apples
(weather demoted cox)
2.
clementines
pears

red onion
courgette
braccoli
grapes
satsumas
strawberrie
kiwis
red pepper
toms x 2
cucumber
lettuce
bananas

REFLECTING BACK, I now realise that I began the collection during a time of considerable stress in my professional life. In 2014, I was hard at work on a large and important grant application, upon which much of the future of the small charitable organisation that I single-handedly ran depended on, as did my livelihood. Or at least that was how it seemed at the time. On receipt of the great news that the grant proposal had been successful, I was then obliged to green light a capital development project in addition to securing the necessary match funds that I had so confidently indicated would be forthcoming on a positive outcome. Thus, further accelerating the work-related stress.

The start of my collecting also coincided with an enormously difficult time on a personal level with tragic events unfolding for my sister, who lived in San Francisco, and which ultimately culminated in her death there in June 2016 (and on the day that the UK voted to leave the European Union). In the aftermath of her death, there were several years of significant fallout, decimating what was left of an already very small, dysfunctional and dispersed family. The pain of this was still foremost in my daily life when, almost precisely a year later, a much-loved young friend and colleague was killed, together with her mother, in the fire at Grenfell Tower.

The activity of collecting, more than the collection itself perhaps, was somehow consoling in all of this. It is widely acknowledged that in the US the massive rise in popularity of collecting apparently valueless or otherwise overlooked stuff of everyday life such as matchbooks, baseball cards, stamps, coins and bottle tops corresponded

LEMONS
LEMONADE
Milk
Loo Roll
TP
Kitchen Towels
Ketchup

with the great depression of the 1930s. Collecting has long been popular in the UK, too. The Ticket and Fare Collection Society (now the Transport Ticket Society) was founded in 1946, a year after the end of the Second World War. It seems to me to be quite natural that, while living amid chaos beyond one's control, it can be a welcome distraction to amass a collection of small, harmless, overlooked and unthreatening bus tickets. They somehow speak to a normality of existence and, when life has become entirely off balance, strangely help to provide equilibrium in the daily routine.

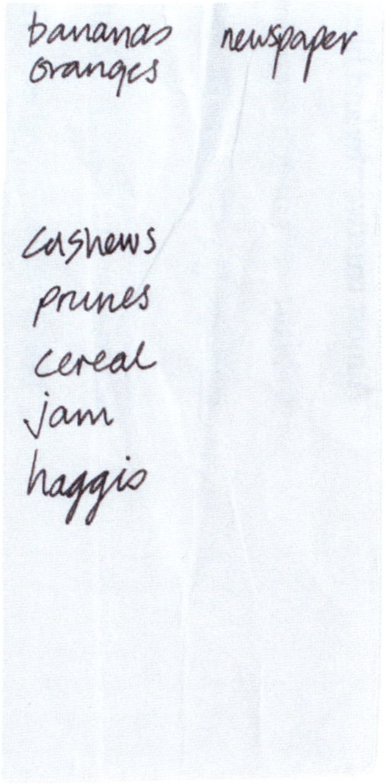
bananas
oranges
newspaper
cashews
prunes
cereal
jam
haggis

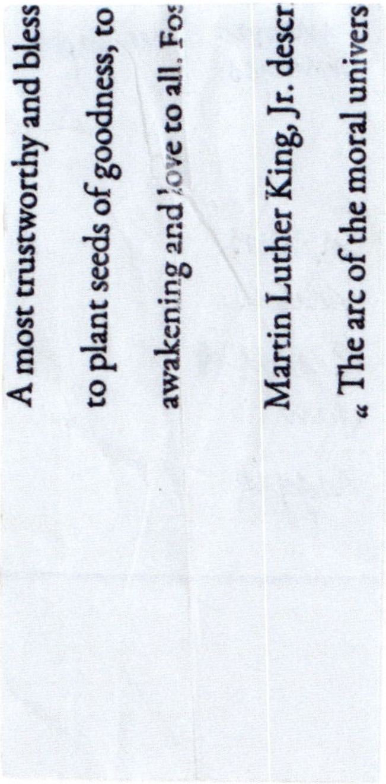
A most trustworthy and bless
to plant seeds of goodness, to
awakening and love to all. Fo
Martin Luther King, Jr. descr
" The arc of the moral univers

fat free Greek yoghurt

melon/fruit

veg

Marmalade

Holiday Kit.

Cash.

~~Foil.~~

~~Cling~~ Film.

~~Ice Cream~~

~~Sugar~~

~~Risotto~~

Kitchen ~~Towels.~~

~~Honey~~

~~Pasta sauce~~

Lamps.

~~Cake~~

~~Toothpaste~~

Pied Piper – Neville Shute.

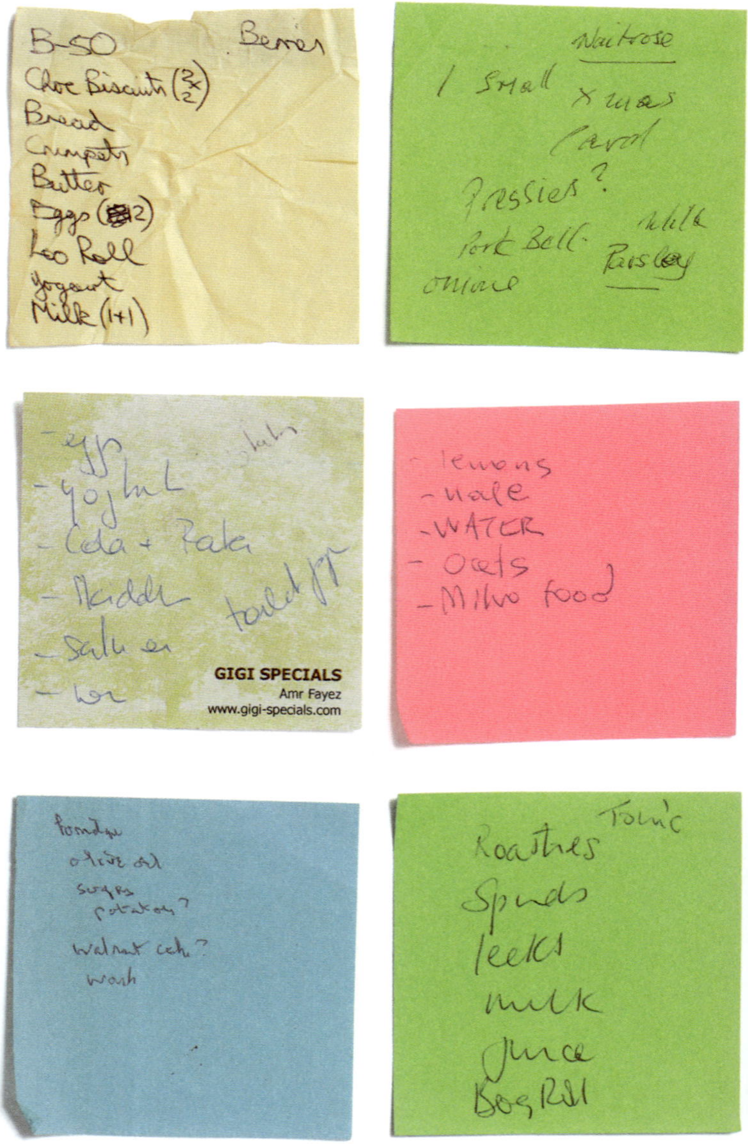
Bread
Butter
Loo Roll
Yogurt
Milk (1+1)
Waitrose
Pressies?
Parsley
GIGI SPECIALS
Amr Fayez
www.gigi-specials.com
- lemons
- WATER
- Milo food
olive oil
potatoes?
Tonic
Roasties
Spuds
leeks
milk
juice
Bog Roll

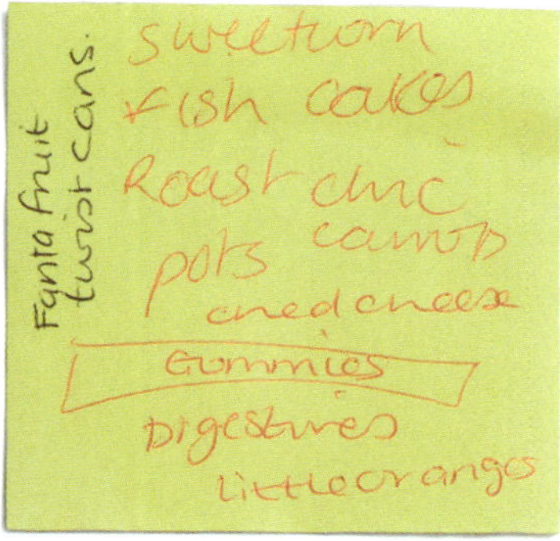
Fanta fruit twist cans.
sweetcorn
fish cakes
Roast chic
pots
carrots
ched cheese
Gummies
Digestives
little oranges

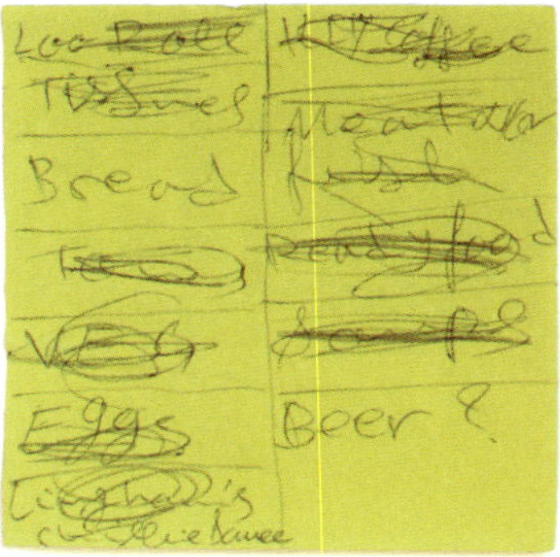
Loo Roll
Bread
Eggs
Beer ?

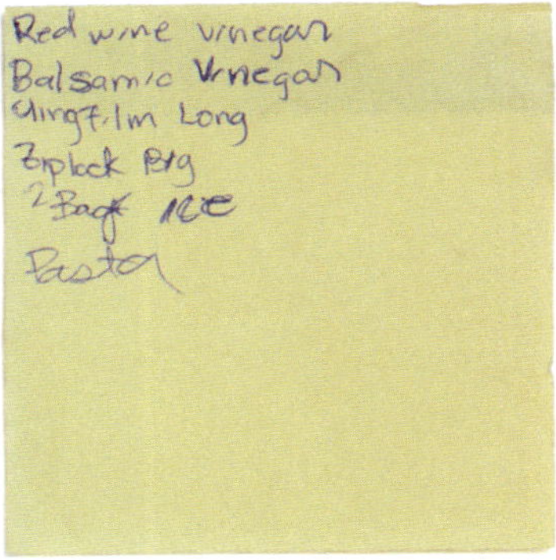
Red wine vinegar
Balsamic Vinegar
Clingfilm Long
Ziplock Bag
2 Bags ICE
Pasta

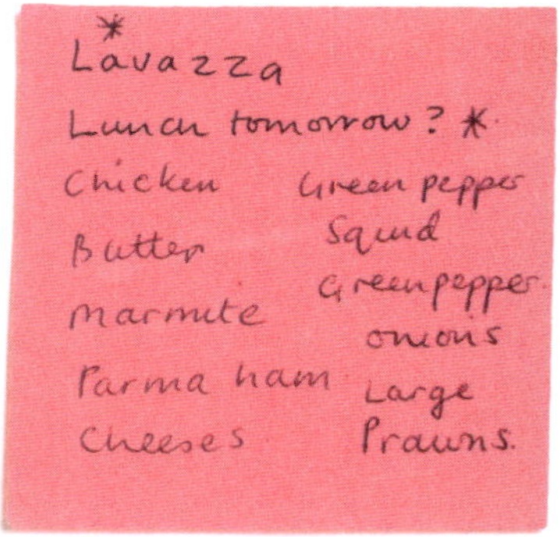
*
Lavazza
Lunch tomorrow? *
Chicken
Butter
marmite
Parma ham
Cheeses
Green pepper
Squid
Green pepper.
onions
Large Prawns.

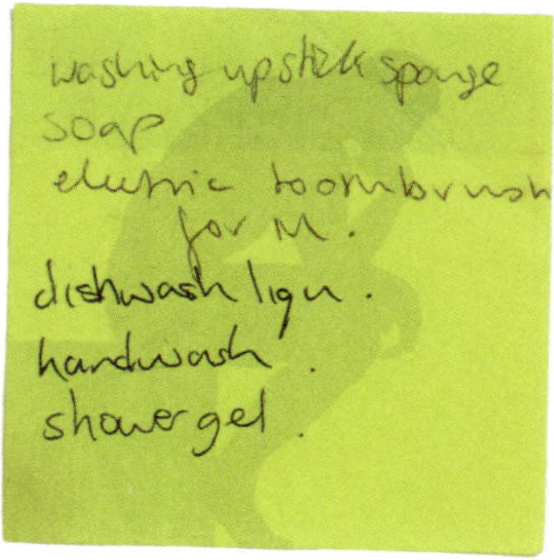
washing up stick sponge
soap
electric toothbrush for M.
dishwash liqu.
handwash.
shower gel.

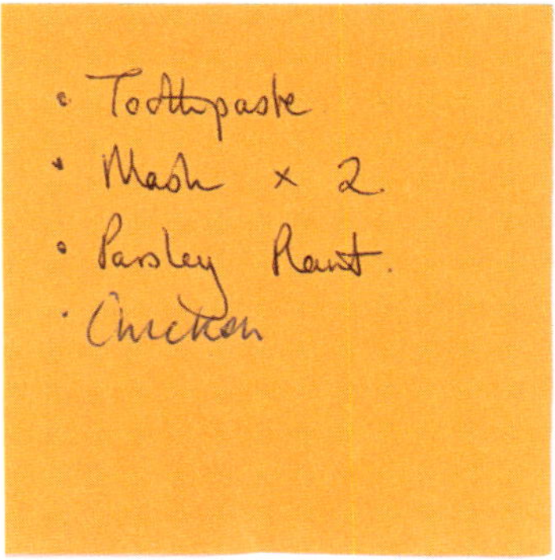
• Toothpaste
• Mash x 2.
• Parsley Plant.
• Chicken

M&CSAATCHI

Lamb
Stuffing

Peas
Cabbage
Cauliflower Cheese
Pots
York Puds

Cox fruit

Cheese
Yogurts

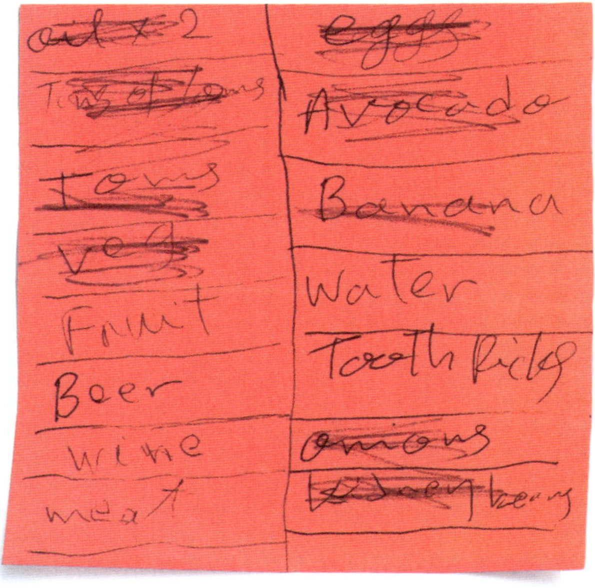

Avocado
Banana
Water
Fruit
Beer
wine
meat
onions
beans

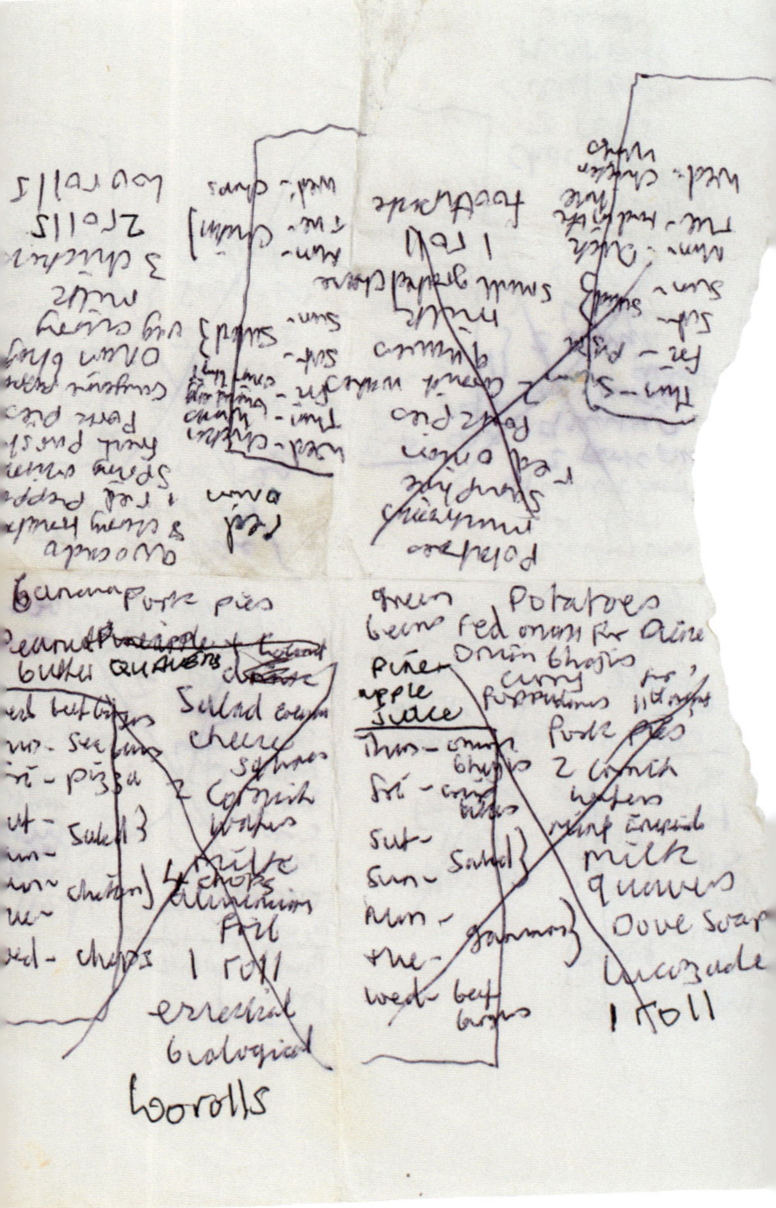
Banana
Pork pies
Peanut butter ~~Pineapple + yoghurt~~
QUAVERS
~~cheese~~
Salad cream
cheese
Scones
2 Cornish wafers
4 milk
4 chops
aluminium foil
1 roll
[illegible] biological
loorolls

Wed - beef burgers
Thurs - [illegible]
Fri - pizza
Sat - } Salad
Sun -
Mon - } chicken
Tue -
Wed - chops

green beans
Pure apple juice

Thurs - onion bhajis
Fri - [illegible]
Sat - } Salad
Sun -
Mon - } gammon
Tue -
Wed - beef burgers

Potatoes
red onions for Aine
Onion bhajis
curry for [illegible]
poppadums
Pork pies
2 Cornish wafers
[illegible]
milk
quavers
Dove soap
Lucozade
1 roll

Potatoes
mushrooms
Samphire
red onion
Pork pies
2 Cornish wafers
quavers
milk
small grated cheese
1 roll
toothpaste

Thurs - S[illegible]
Fri - Pizza
Sat - } Salad
Sun -
Mon - Duck
Tue - toad in the hole
Wed - chicken wings

red onion
avocado
8 cherry tomatoes
1 red pepper
Spring onions
fresh parsley
Pork pies
Cayenne pepper
onion bhajis
veg curry
milk
3 chickens
2 rolls
loo rolls

Wed - chicken
Thurs - [illegible]
Fri - [illegible]
Sat - } Salad
Sun -
Mon - } Chicken
Tue -
Wed - chops

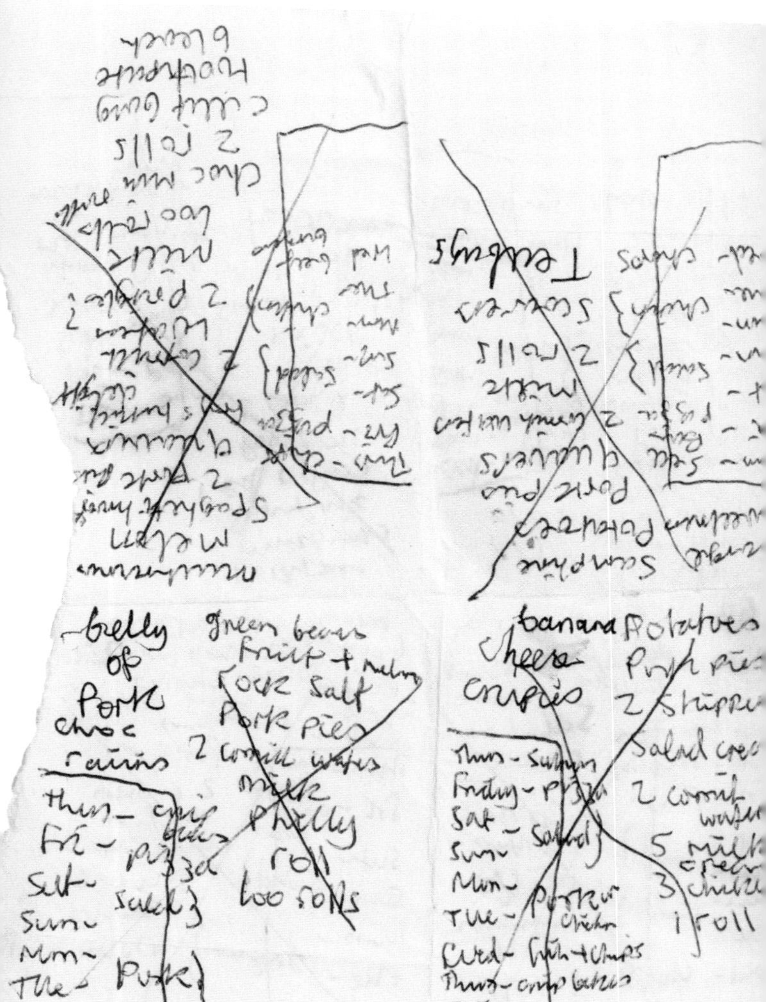

belly of Pork
choc raisins
green beans
fruit + nutmeg
rock salt
Pork pies
2 cornish wafers
milk
Philly
roll
loo rolls
Thurs – crisp bakes
Fri – pizza
Sat – salad
Sun –
Mon –
Tue – Pork
Wed – chops
banana
Potatoes
Cheese
crispies
Pork pies
2 cornish wafers
5 milk
cream
3 chicken
1 roll
Thurs – salmon
Friday – pizza
Sat – salad
Sun –
Mon –
Tue – Porker chicken
Wed – fish + chips
Thurs – crisp bakes
Fri –

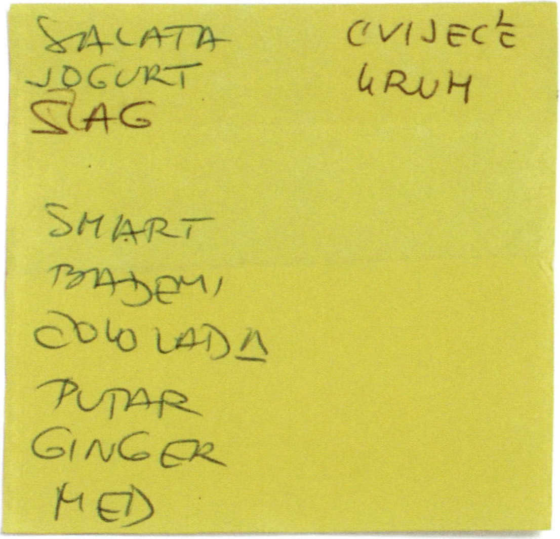
SALATA
JOGURT
ŠLAG
SMART
BADEMI
ČOKOLADA
PUTAR
GINGER
MED
CVIJEĆE
KRUH

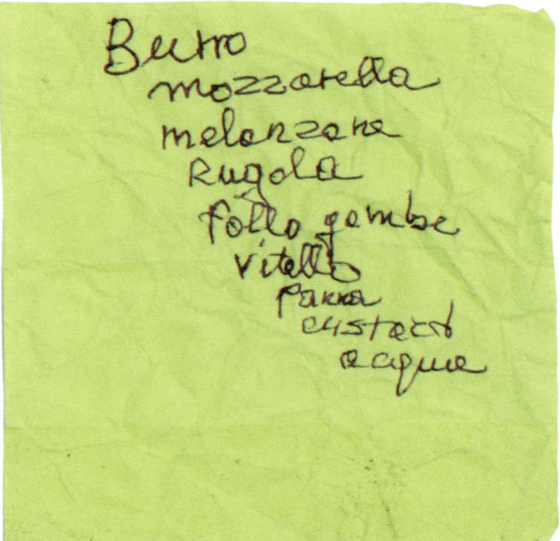
Burro
mozzarella
melanzane
Rugola
Pollo gambe
vitello
Panna
crostata
acqua

Tea

Mushrooms

Eggs

Hashbrowns

Bacon / Sausages

Beans

Croissants

Sourdough bread

Shoji Paper?

- C-battery
- Light Bulbs

Vincent van Gogh
Four sunflowers gone to seeds, 1887

300g pine nuts ?
Parsley.
basil
Rosemary.
fresh breadcrumbs
500g ricotta
4 lemons
eggs.
1k mince beef.

Quorn.
Tomatoes
Salad
bread
Mozzarella

5x 400g TOMS
~~450g C. Sugar~~
450g ground Almonds

SAGE

~~MILK~~

Canadian
stoneground.
WHOLEMEAL

Bakon

OIL

Carrotts

~~Bread~~

Burgers – ordinary

Banana's

BY AUTUMN 2017, the collection had grown to approximately 600 lists. Until this point – perhaps related to the grieving process – it had been important for me to keep it a low-key and private recreation. I had enjoyed the degree of clandestineness and the absurd level of gravitas that not sharing it with others permitted. This felt appropriate at a time when the reality of death was too difficult to grasp.

But now, with a substantial number accumulated, I was gradually beginning to want to share them. While a handful of lists could be a curiosity – but not, ultimately, that remarkable – several hundred were an amount to be contended with. Something to get amongst, as it were. I began to show them to a few trusted friends who I hoped would understand why I found them so appealing. These tentative outings were met with enthusiastic feedback, and so I was emboldened to share the collection more widely.

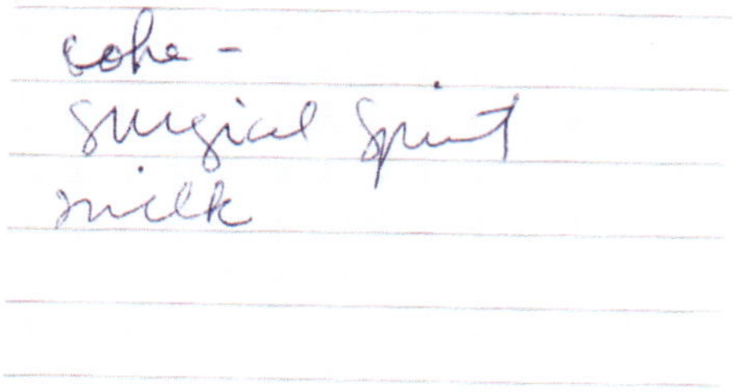
coke -
surgical spirit
milk

I submitted a proposal to include the collection in the one-day Table Top Museum exhibition at the Art Workers' Guild in Bloomsbury, London, on 24 September. The proposal, which also became the description used on the exhibition handout, read:

SHOPPING LIST MUSEUM – N7 6PA

572 lists from Waitrose Holloway Road, gathered since 2014. Readymade meets concrete poetry meets domestic haiku. Richly textured, discarded primary source materials towards an unempirical analysis into north London food consumption and mores.

SCallops
Sardines
Bread
Broc (2)
Soup
PorridGe

I was delighted to have my proposal accepted, which was one of 22 collections and installations from coffee grinders and paperweights to gay dolls and coastal curiosities.

Keen to keep the visitor experience an intimate one, I invested in a dozen robust black presentation folders, enabling visitors to individually rifle through and absorb the contents at their leisure. I was impressed by how long people spent looking intensely through folder after folder.

Scallops
Sardines
Bread
Broc (2)
Soup
Porridge

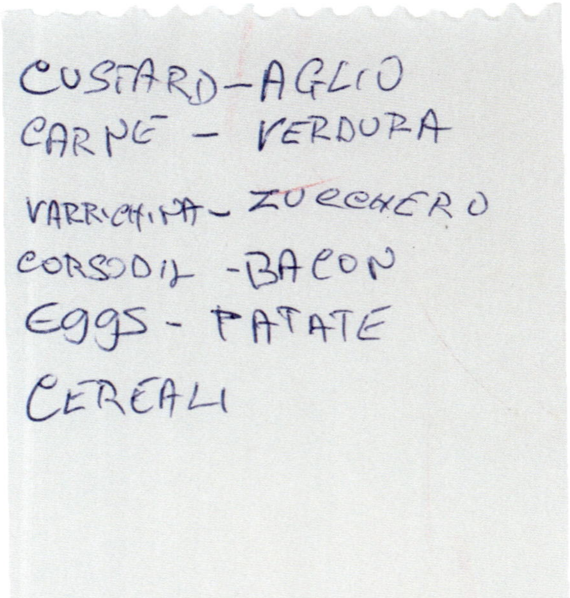
CUSTARD-AGLIO
CARNE - VERDURA
VARRICHINA- ZUCCHERO
CORSODIL -BACON
EGGS - PATATE
CEREALI

FISH - 2 MILK
BREAD - BUTTER
SPHETTI - SOUP
VEG - WATER
BLUEBERRYS
KRUMS - HAM
ICECREAM RICE

Eggs
tonic/juice
vodka/red wine
bread
Sponge
chicken
Egg tagliatelle
creme fraich

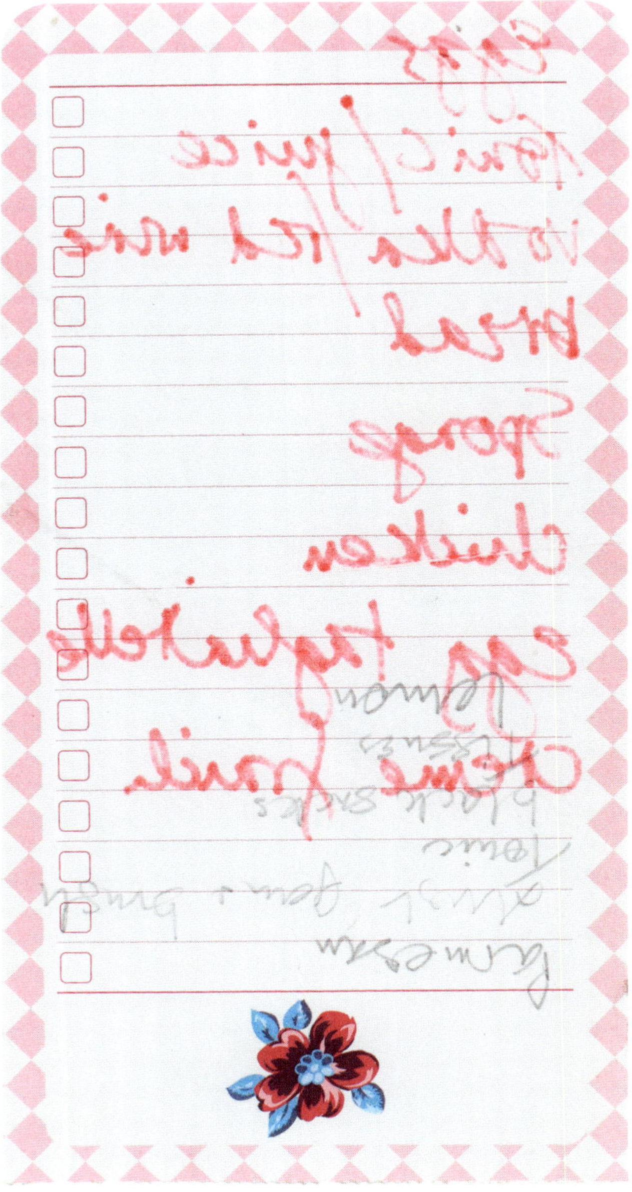
eggs
tonic / juice
vodka / red wine
bread
sponge
chicken
egg tagliatelle
lemon
tissues
creme fraiche
black sacks
tonic
parmesan

Fan mail

WAITROSE

Chicken Wings
Legs

Potatoes

Peas

Dessert

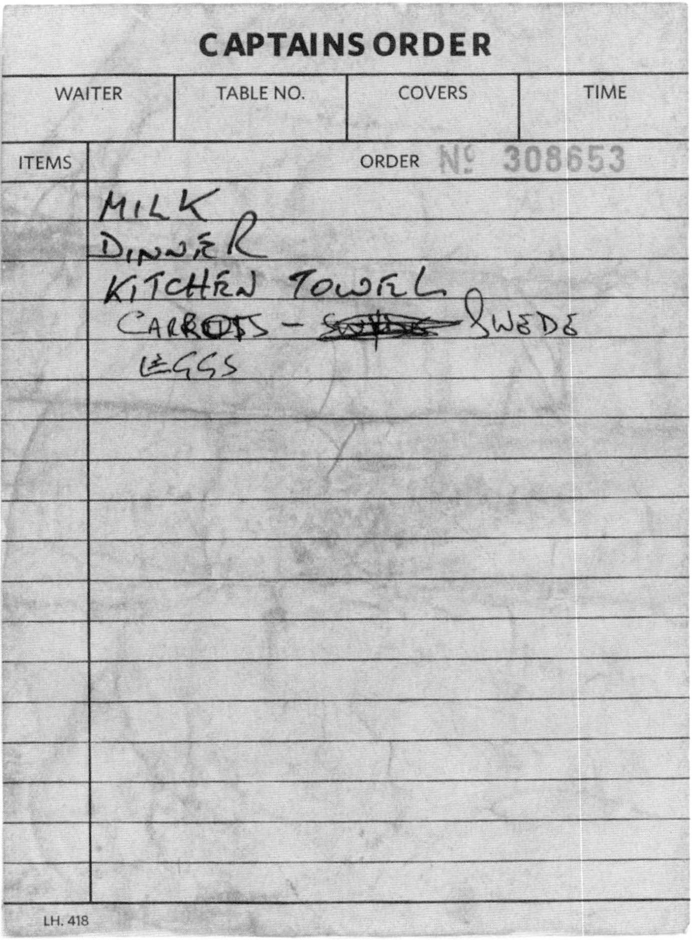

CAPTAINS ORDER

WAITER	TABLE NO.	COVERS	TIME

ITEMS ORDER Nº 308653

MILK
DINNER
KITCHEN TOWEL
CARROTS – ~~[illegible]~~ SWEDE
EGGS

LH. 418

Toilet roll
pasta spagetti +
green sponges
cif cream cleanser
juice
Earl Grey Tea
Pukka night time tea
parmesan
brown sugar
kitchen towel
juice

eggs, -
fish Flash Liquid
tomato risotto
pheasants - kitchen roll
week
nice noodles. medium
stir fry
garlic -
bagels 2
tomato soup
cream cheese

Earl Grey / Builders
Golden Morsel cheese
dishwasher tablets rice cakes
vegetables. brown carrot courgette
spinach
Salad - teacakes
Grapefruit
yoghurt
porridge/cereals
teacakes - sliced loaf
biscuits juice toilet paper
Ecover washing Powder
non-toxic weed / squirt + Mop floor cleaner brown

eggs
Fish Flash Liquid
tomato risotto
phasola - fritte
week yol
rice noodles, melon
stir fry
garlic
bagels
tomato soup
Cream cheese
Earl Grey // Buddha
Gilden Metal cheese
tablets rice cakes
dish washer
Vegetable, brown carrot courgette spinach
Salad - tomatoes
Grapefruit
yoghurt
porridge oats
tea cakes - sli bar
biscuits toilet paper
Ecover washing Powder
non-toxic wood/carpet + floor clean bar

Mayo

More buns

Citrus

Crisps etc

Outdoor lights

~~Doorbell~~

More apples.

~~Double Sided Sticky Tape~~

Batteries

~~Morning~~

Evening lovely!

Hope you had a good day.

Thanks again for having me – slept like a log as per.

Washing's on!

Can't wait to see you on friday – let me know if you need me to do anything to help other than keywatch

love!

xxx

Red peppers
Spring onions
parsley – lots
mint – lots
Lemons
Limes
White onions
White cabbage
large carrots
vac pack beetroot x 3
4 x garlic bulbs

~~Mayonnaise~~
~~– Hellmanns light~~.
Total 2% Greek x 3
lean lamb mince x 2
nice sausages
organic beef mince (LEAN
raw prawns
squid tubes
4 tins of tinned octopus

Brioche buns or large burger buns
Finger rolls
Delfin spray
~~pitta bread~~
aluminium foil
baking parchment.
beer – for darren + Peter
↳ perhaps a 12 pack San miguel
↳ same sam adams
Dishwasher tabs
Deodorant
2 big packs self lighting charcoal
Wood for the chiminea
Shampoo
Bleach

Dairy	Vegetables	Fruit
Milk x 1 [illegible]	Potato	Orange x 1
~~Butter~~	Parsnip	~~Grapefruit~~
~~Flora~~	Broccoli	Banana
Cheese	Cauliflower	Grape
Yoghurt	Courgette	Apple
Eggs	Corn	~~Pear~~
Juice	~~Spinach~~	Strawberry
Crème fraiche	~~Pepper~~	Raspberry
Humus	~~Green beans~~	Blueberry
Tsatsiki	~~Mange touts~~	Blackberry
Tarama	~~Carrots~~	~~Lychees~~
	Carrots (baby)	~~Kiwi~~
	Mushrooms	~~Pineapple~~
	~~Cucumber~~	~~Lemon~~
	~~Tomatoes~~	Cherries
	~~Lettuce~~	~~Lychees~~
	~~Radish~~	~~Pomegranate~~
	~~Aubergines~~	~~Mango~~
	Brussel sprout	~~Dates~~
	~~Red Cabbage~~	

SOAP

at/Fish	Household	Other
~~dines~~	~~Soap~~	Bread (+ pitta)
~~pers~~	~~Bionsen~~	Pasta
~~(+Iceland...)~~		~~Rice~~
~~mon~~		~~Beans~~
oked/salmon x 1		Cooking wine
a		~~Oil~~
k		~~Vinegar~~
cken LES		~~Corn Flour~~
~~cken breast~~		Teas
ab		~~Spices~~
f		~~Herbs~~
n ✓ 1		~~Cereal~~
on ✓ 1		~~Mayonnaise~~
~~mi~~		TACO MIX
~~cetta~~		FAJITA
~~ssels~~		ICE CREAM
~~sages~~		
k		
ak		PIZZA
~~gers~~		
ckerel		

Kitchen foil
500 turkey mince
Onion
Carrot
150g mushrooms
parmesan
2x courgettes
Ice.
Deodorant.

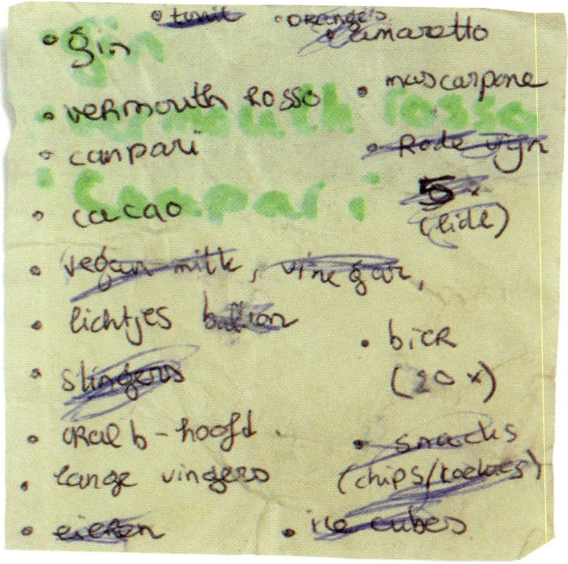

- ~~tonic~~
- ~~oranges~~
- ~~amaretto~~
- gin
- vermouth rosso
- campari
- cacao
- ~~vegan milk~~, ~~vinegar~~,
- lichtjes ~~ballon~~
- ~~slingers~~
- oral b - hoofd
- lange vingers
- ~~eieren~~
- mascarpone
- ~~Rode wijn~~ ~~5x (liter)~~
- bier (20x)
- ~~snacks (chips/koekjes)~~
- ~~ice cubes~~

Gin
…mouth rosso
Campari

toothpaste x 3
milk x 3 + LL
greek yog
b. beans
t. soup
jazz
carrots
bags > 7.5x7.5
~~pencils~~
lamy cartridges
chicken
f. bird
scissors
glue sticks

SWISS

UNIVERSALLY AND SPONTANEOUSLY, it appears that the twentieth century spawned a huge variety of different kinds of collectors of everyday items of minimal or no value. While many of these collections have remained personal and are housed in boxes in a cupboard, the attic or garden shed, other collectors have come together to share their passion and create membership groups. As one would perhaps expect, these have often reflected aspects of national identity. Examples in the UK include the British Beermat Collectors Society (founded 1960), the British Brick Society (founded 1972), the members' newsletter Milk Bottle News (founded 1984) and, in Norway, the Sardine Can Labels Club, which is also a museum (founded in 1987).

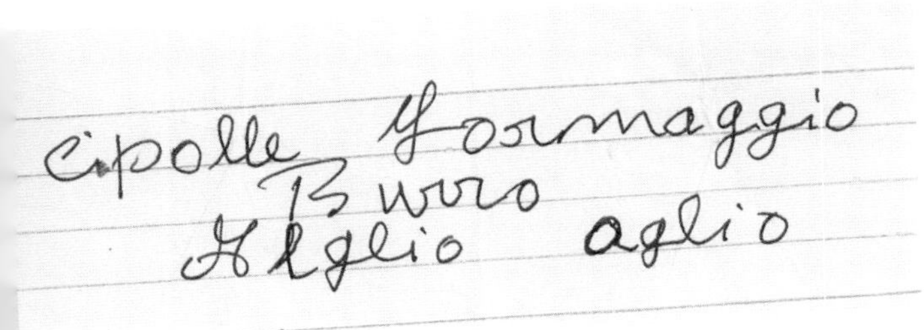
Cipolle
Formaggio
Burro
aglio

Ephemera is a word that has sometimes been associated with shopping list collection. Maurice Rickards, founder of the Ephemera Society in the UK in 1975, and the author of the *Encyclopaedia of Ephemera*, posthumously published in 2000, defined ephemera as 'the minor transient

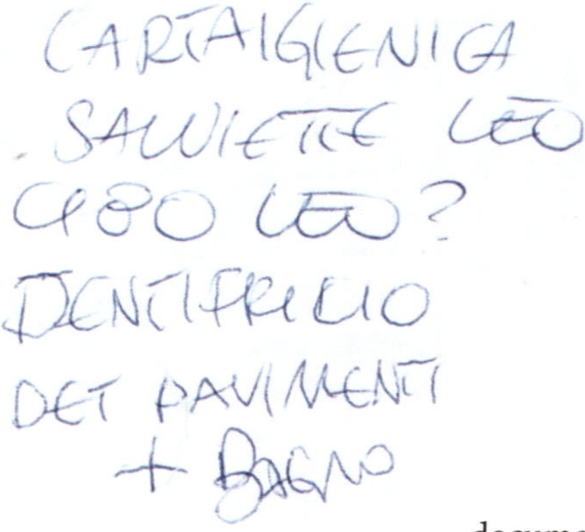
CARTAIGIENICA
SALVIETTE LEO
CIBO LEO?
DENTIFRICIO
DET PAVIMENTI
+ BAGNO

documents of everyday life'. It is a term used to describe printed or handwritten material that, though meant to be thrown away, possesses small and often significant fragments of information that enriches our wider knowledge of historical culture and society. Rickards elevated the study of ephemera into an academic discipline and established the Centre for Ephemera Studies at Reading University in 1993.

While other shopping list collectors might be comfortable with the term, I sense that it ties the lists down too much, restricting their potential enjoyment to a reading that wants them to be defined and fixed. I worry that the label of 'ephemera' might diminish the possibility for the lists to exist simply as they are, untethered from their authors. I would prefer for the texts to have the potential to be read as unexpected, random word (dis-)associations, perhaps like nonsense or found poetry. The scraps or sheets of paper that they are written on also bring additional qualities and merits that encourage a more haptic relationship with the object. Many of the backs of the lists are to me as important as the fronts.

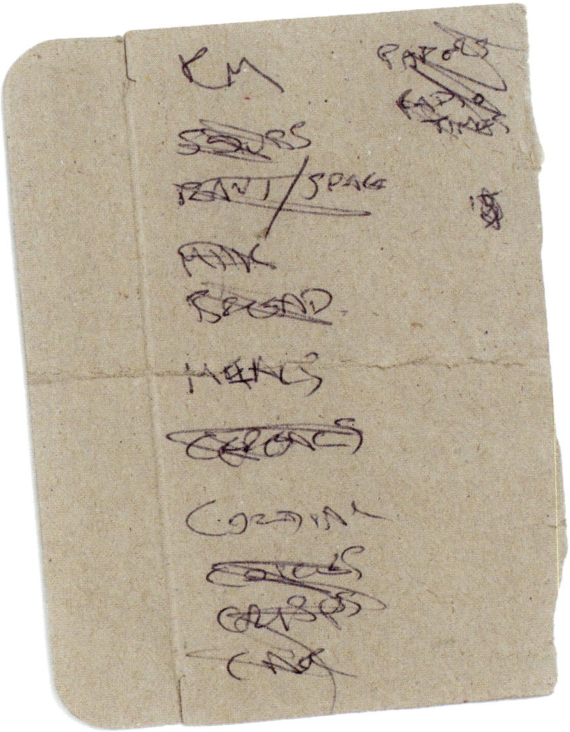

Pork
Loin
Fruit
Veg = Broci
Rice
Water X2
E—Cigs

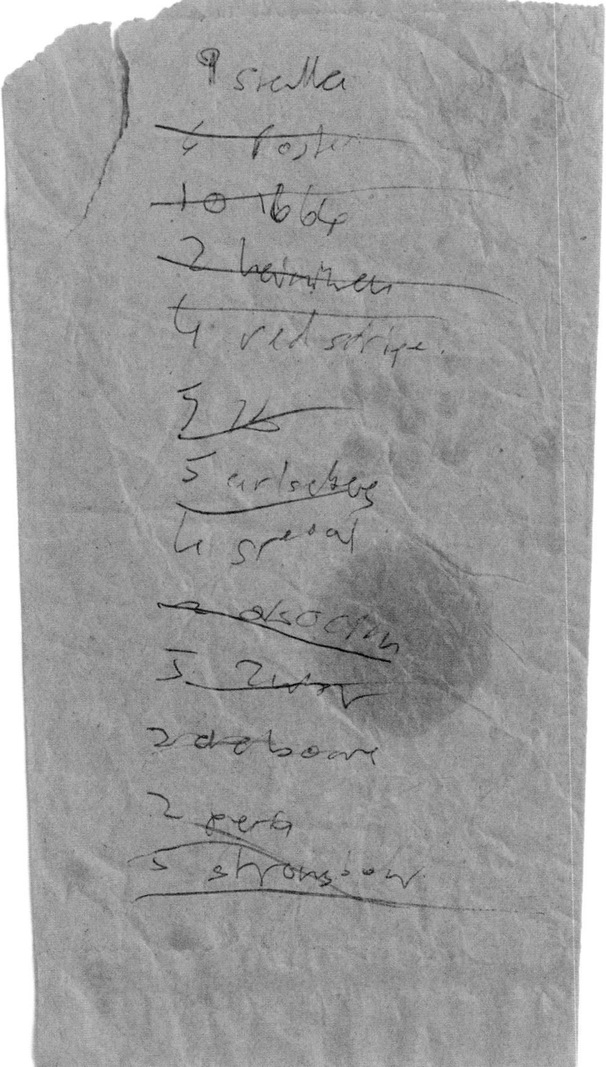

9 stella
~~4 foster~~
~~10~~ 1664
~~2 heineken~~
~~4~~ red stripe.
~~5 [illegible]~~
5 carlsberg
4 special
~~2 [illegible]~~
~~5 [illegible]~~
2 [illegible]
2 peroni
~~5 strongbow~~

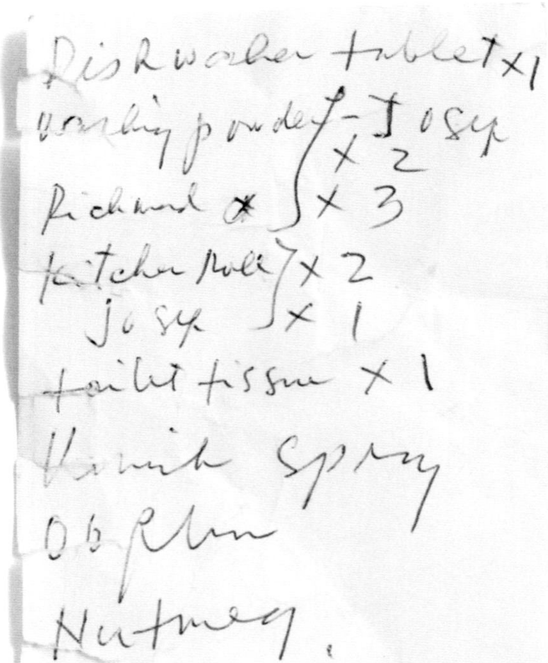
Dishwasher tablet x1
washing powder – Josep x 2
Richard ✱ x 3
kitchen roll x 2
Josep x 1
toilet tissue x 1
Varnish spray
Ob Rhm
Nutmeg.
all spice

>milk
>eggs
>chopped tomatoes
>spaghetti
>mince for bolognaise
>chicken / ? for risotto
>onions
>carrots
>potatoes
>lemons
> limes
>butter
>brocolli
>green beans
>smoked haddock
>chillis
>garlic
>parsley
>coriander
>parmesan
> ketchup
>tonic
>gherkins
>nanal
>marigolds
>bread flour.

>1 bramley apple (or similar)
>chips
>beet

HiLifide Tuna
Eggs
Butter 2
Flora
~~Cheese~~
HAm / Tounge
Sordines
Soups
Potatoes
Tangerins
Apples
Grapes
Rasberrys / Strawbergs
Pears
Broccolli
Fostes
Wine
Scotch Eggs
Pea Nuts

Iceland
Chips
Cat Food ?

Tomatoes
Cucumber
Red Salmon
Eclairs
Frozen Fis

MArks CArd (30)

Water

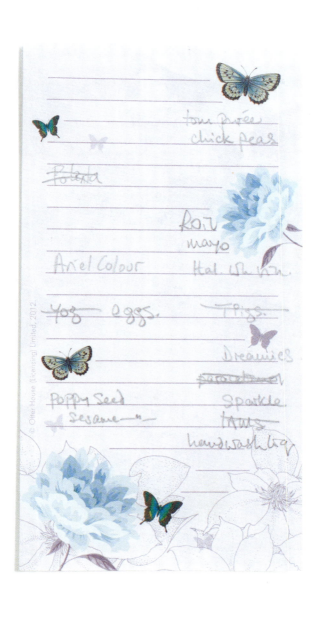

tom purée
chick peas

~~Polenta~~

Roti
mayo

Ariel Colour
Hal. wh. wn.

~~Yog~~ eggs.
~~Figs.~~

Dreamies

~~paracetamol~~

Poppy Seed
Sparkle
Sesame "
~~tabs~~
handwash liq

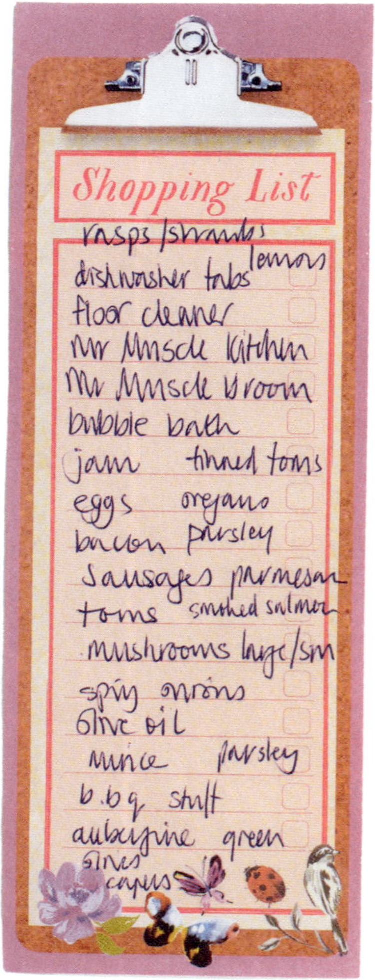
Shopping List
rasps/strawbs
lemons
dishwasher tabs
floor cleaner
Mr Muscle kitchen
Mr Muscle broom
bubble bath
jam tinned toms
eggs oregano
bacon parsley
sausages parmesan
toms smoked salmon
mushrooms large/sm
spring onions
olive oil
mince parsley
b.b.q stuff
aubergine green
olives
capers

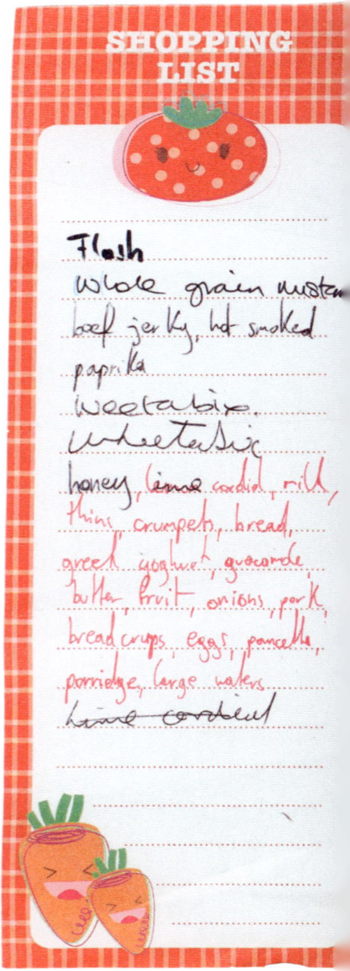
SHOPPING LIST
Flash
whole grain mustard
beef jerky, hot smoked
paprika
weetabix
wheetabix
honey, lime cordial, rill,
thins, crumpets, bread,
greek yoghurt, guacamole,
butter, fruit, onions, pork,
bread crumbs, eggs, panchetta,
porridge, large waters
lime cordial

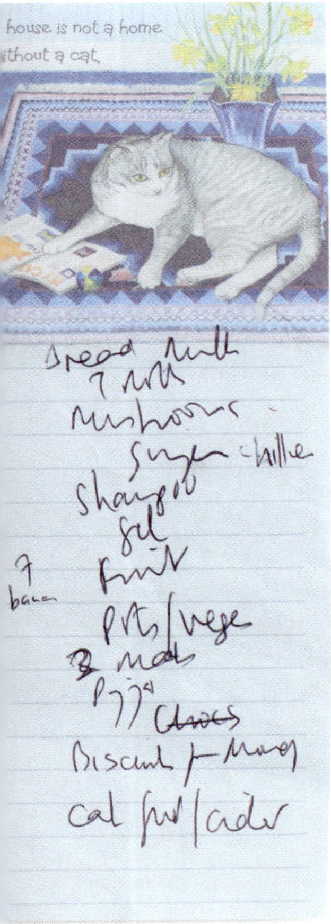
house is not a home
ithout a cat

Bread Milk
? Milk
Mushrooms
Sugar chillie
Shampoo
gel
7 banan Fruit
Pots/vege
meats
Pizza
~~Cheese~~
Biscuits for Mary
Cat food/cider

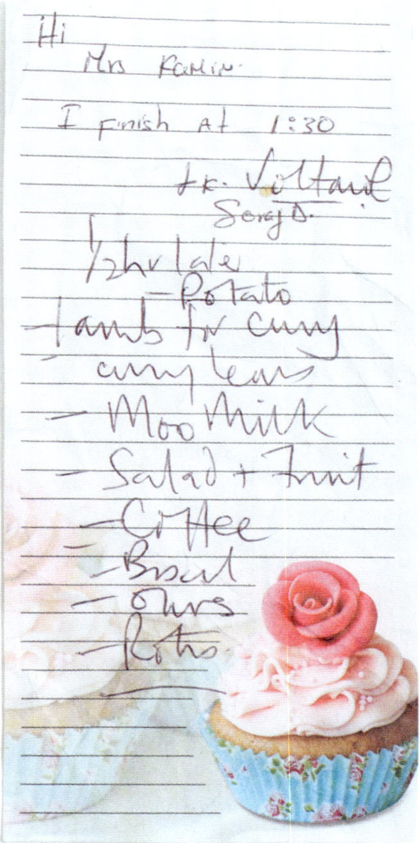

Hi
Mrs Ramin
I finish at 1:30
fr. Voltaire
Seraj D.
½ hr late
– Potato
Lamb for curry
curry leaves
– Moo Milk
– Salad + Fruit
– Coffee
– Biscuit
– Others
– Rotis

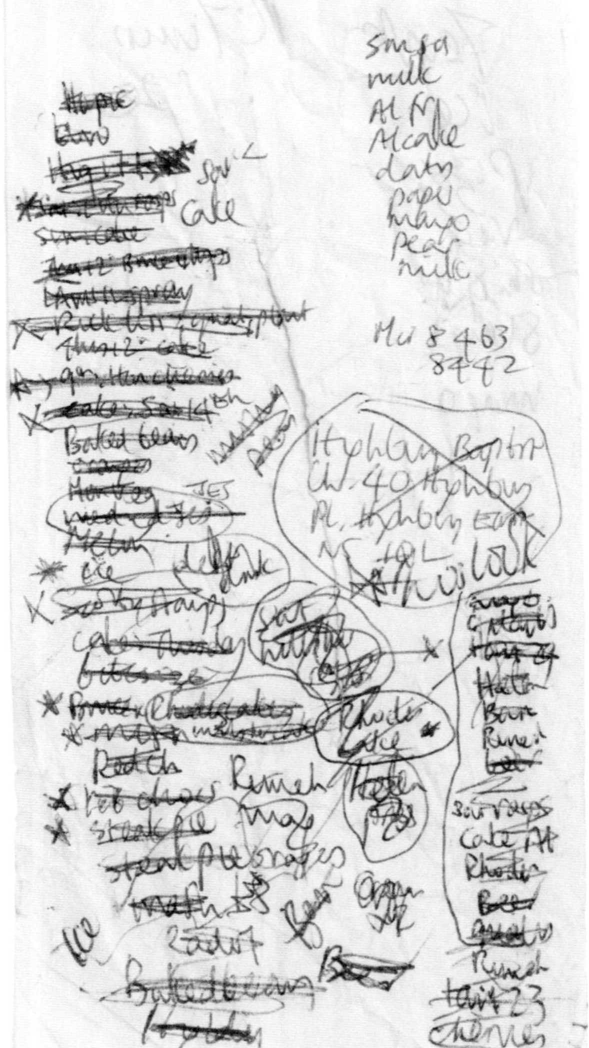
smga
milk
Al fr
Al cake
dates
papa
mango
pear
milk

Mu 8 463
8442

Highbury Baptist
Ch. 40 Highbury
Pl, Highbury East
N5 1QL

cake
Baked beans
Rhodes cake
Rumah
sausages
cake
Rhodes
Rumah
cherries

Tart R Tums
ice pear
pizza
veg
sm g y
stays
mayo

- iron ✓
- cucumber ✓
- tea bags ✓
- kitchen roll ✓
- pasta ✓
- dish washer tablets ✓
- peas ✓
- cereal ✓
- sugar ✓
- flour ✓
- eggs ✓
- bananas ✓
- apples ✓
- brocoli ✓
- walnuts ✓
- feta ✓
- rolls ✓
- stirfry ✓
- beansprouts ✓
- mushrooms ✓
- beef ✓
- chicken ✓
- potatoes ✓
- ham salad ✓
- bagels ✓
- crisps ✓
- candles ✓
- floor polish
- strain drinks ✓
- baked beans ✓

- washing
- ironing
- change bed
- clean food cupboards
- Santa do

SHOPPING
LIST

49½
12
61½

Shopping

paper.

cat food / dried food.

cat litter.

eco-rubbish sacks.

rubbish sacks.

spray (not RAID)

milk

yoghurt

SUNDAY –

MONDAY.

TUESDAY

FRIDAY –

little milks

coffee.

oats

cereal.

marmite.

long-life milk

tropicana.

fruit / veg.

soups

WAITROSE

milk
bread.
eggs
rolls.
veg: – green beans (org.)

TURK

[illegible]

From: [illegible]
Sent: 14 February 2014 14:27
To: [illegible]
Subject: Food

Do you fancy a chunky minestrone soup for Sat tea/dinner? I'm assuming we'll have eaten a largish lunch and so may only want something light. Freya could have it on Sunday too....

You can bake some bread Sat afternoon when we get home to go with it?

I can't face going out again with Freya this afternoon as it's so nasty out there. Would you mind popping to Waitrose from the bus at all? I reckon we can get all our weekend food tonight which would be nice. The below includes what we need for the oxtail stew (plus sides) and sat night dinner:

Blue milk
salad leaves
leeks x2
big bag of kale (to have with oxtail stew and minestrone)
red onions x2
carrots x2
cucumber
fennel
green beans or runner beans (for Freya)
sprouting broccoli (There should be courgettes in the minestrone but i thought the stalks and heads of sprouting broc could be a good seasonal replacement?)
celery - BUT only if you can face it in the minestrone?
pancetta
proper chicken stock
tin PLUM toms x3
cannellini or barlotti beans
red wine for cooking
Sar Lindt
Digestif tea

+ Any bread baking ingredients if you're going to do a sat night loaf
+anything you want for lunch on sunday - ham?

Does that sound ok?

Thanks baby xx

[redacted]

From:	[redacted]
Sent:	16 May 2014 17:29
To:	[redacted]
Subject:	shoppin

Please...

Ripe avocado (usually pack of two)
Nice bread
Fresh mint
Spring onions
1 pack tomatoes
1 bag salad
Pot of salad thing(s) such as couscous/whatever
Small bunch of flowers for their room (if you can manage it!)

FANKS

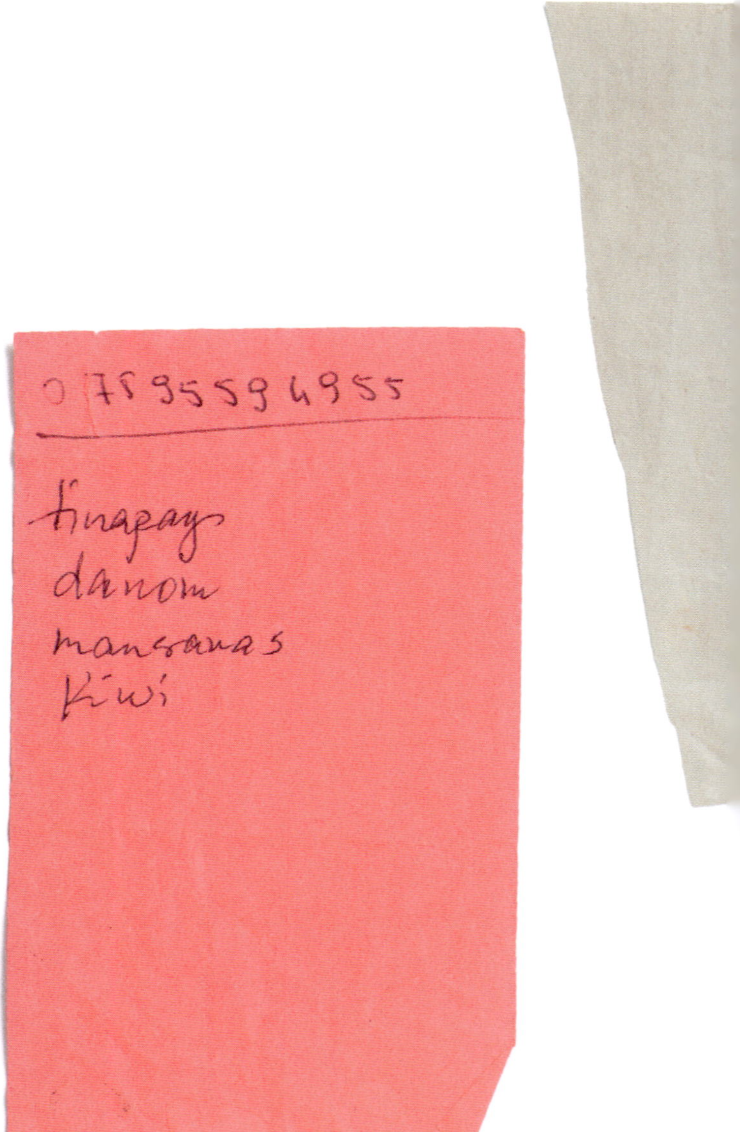
0 75 95559 4955

Tinapay
danom
mansanas
Kiwi

Dishwashing
Tablets

Cat food.

Pay Postage

Natwest

Humous —

Halloumi —

Cucumber —

- tomates | Pdt.
- Poires
- oranges Bio
- Citrons Bio
- epinards
- Courgettes -
- mandarines - Pesto
- charcuterie -
- fromage
- sucre
- farine ++
- jus de fruits
- Salade -
- ~~[illegible]~~ - crumpets
- Beurre (?) - yaourts
- javel - PQ
- viande
- papier cadeau -

+++

- PQ sachet [illegible]

Biscuits

Καρτα
Πατατες
φρουτα
φοινίκια
Tripl
Ultra So
FSC

(16) Maybe a cheesecake

(17) FISH.

(18) FRUIT.

CEO · IMPACT EXCHANGE

SHOPPING LIST

(15) pasta maybe?

1. Bulbs
2. flash wooden floor
3. Rice
4. Custard
5. tinned tomatoes chopped.
6. Toilet Rolls...
7. Butter
8. Cream.
9. Cling Film
10. yogurt
11. choc
12. toothpaste
13. BREAD loads of it
14. cereal (country crisp!)

JAMIE'S BARMITZVAH

Viakal

Shreddies

Squash

Kitchen towel

Unsalted butter

Chocolate x 2

Eggs

Golden Syrup?

Caster Sugar

Small plain flour

22/23 MARCH 2014

[illegible]

[illegible]

~~Tuna tins Waitrose~~

~~Anchor Spreadable~~
Yeo Valley ~~Buttery~~ Spread

~~Wasabi~~

~~Maris Piper 1.55~~
~~Almonds~~ ~~Broccoli~~
~~Carrots~~
~~Baby Tomatoes~~ ~~12 Eggs~~
~~Apples~~
~~Bananas~~ ~~Berries~~
~~Pancakes~~
~~Bagels~~ ~~Clementines~~
~~Croissants~~
~~Poilane Sliced~~ ~~Bacon~~
~~crispbread crackers~~
~~Non Bio Capsules~~
~~Happy Faces~~
~~Frozen Chips~~
~~Frozen Fries~~
~~Ketchup~~

~~Milk~~

Yoghurt – Greek
Vanilla Activia
Straight Up
~~Chocolate Mousses~~
~~Apple Juice~~
~~Vodka~~

Waitrose

organic chicken

cat food

Kitchen Roll

Soya milk

Butter

pasta chicken nuggets food

Waitrose Duchy Organic Butter

corn thins.

good olive oil

balsamic vinegar.

capers / green beans

honey

Waitrose toilet duck x 2

mayonnaise

ham / pastrami

tea / slimline tonic water

diet coke

Bertolli olive spread.

Market / Veg Stall Essex Road

small tomatoes. (lots)

green beans

flat white peaches.

lettuce (both)

rocket.

carrots.

potatoes.

lemons.

courgettes (lots).

Superdrug.

Slimfast
Bars

~~[illegible]~~

Waitrose.

Tripe Stick
Sausages
Desert
Cat food
Ovaltine

~~[illegible]~~

Jacket-
Potatoes

MY FRIEND, THE ARTIST and writer Erica Van Horn, did not send me her found list (which, due to my self-imposed rules, could not in any event form part of my collection), but I was delighted that instead she shared her diary entry about it.

29 JANUARY, TUESDAY

I am always pleased to find a lost shopping list.
I like the sort of eavesdropping effect of reading
what somebody else intends to purchase.
Yesterday I found a small piece of cardboard.

The list read:

Rolls/TV Guide
Buns for Norman.
Chicken.

I spent the rest of the day thinking about Buns for
Norman Chicken.
I repeated it over and over again. It became a little chant.

Buns for Norman Chicken!

I was delighted with the name Norman Chicken.

I woke up happy, with the name Norman Chicken
on my tongue. Now I see that Norman Chicken is
neither a person nor a recipe. Buns for Norman was
one thing. And then there was Chicken.

Tomatoe purée.
kitchen towels..
~~HA~~ Chocolate.
milk.
dinner tonight.
dinner tomorrow.
saturday night.
gin ½ bottle.
wine.
Ham.
Smoked salmon.
Frozen peas.
Veges.

876 WE

14:30 TOIL

12:30

σερβιέττες

— ροζό [illegible] — αμύγδαλα

— γιόνια + σαπούνια

— q-tips

— φαγητά [illegible]

— [illegible]

— ρόζλιε + αμύγδαλα

— [illegible] [illegible]

— [illegible] Ελλ[illegible]

[illegible] σερβιέττες

ZAKUPY

- DO TOALETY PŁYN
- PORRIDGE - GOLDEN SYRUP.
- MASŁO /
- PARMESAN
- DYNIA
- NAPKINS
- SHALLOT
- MS+ ORANGE JUICE
- SHORTBREAD.
- MOŻE LODY

20:30 - BBC 2

POLAK - DRAGONS DEN

Bin liners
White bin liners
Fairy clothes
Quinces
Yoghurts
Chicken pieces
Pork chops
Bacon -
Quince
Cheese
Walnuts
Quince
Ham

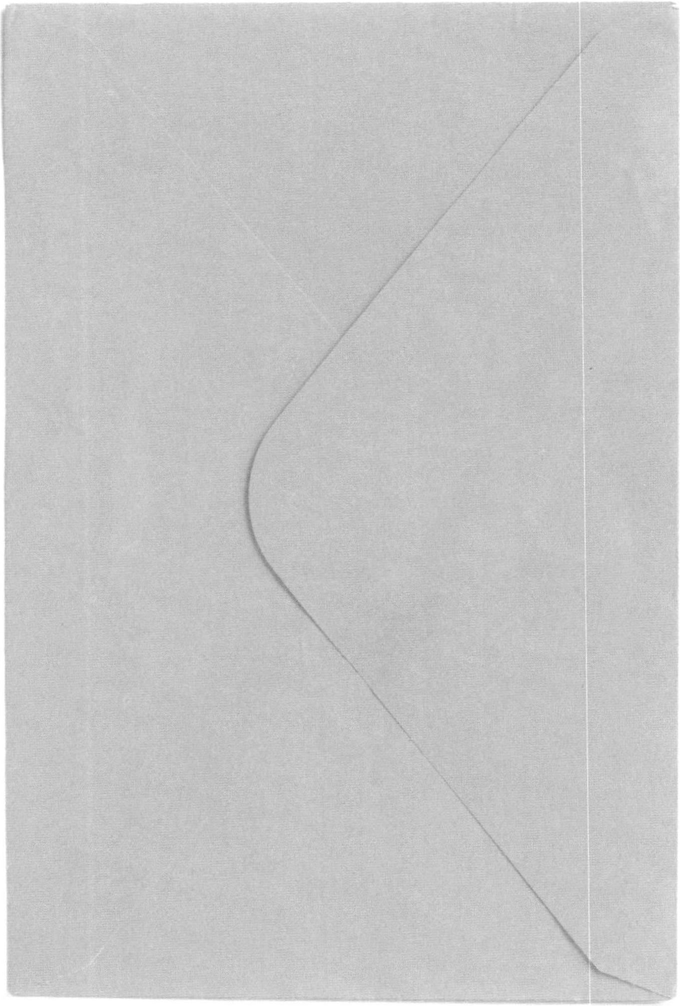

RIZ

~~MILK~~

~~Onion~~

eggs

~~NORMAL Ketchup~~

~~asparagus~~

Brown Tape

2016

October

Friday 28

VOVA SALCICIA

FORMAGIO POLLO

PATATE S. PELEGRINO

SALE PASTA

FENEL

TOMATO

HAM

October						2016
M	T	W	T	F	S	S
31					1	2
3	4	5	6	7	8	9
10	11	12	13	14	15	16
17	18	19	20	21	22	23
24	25	26	27	28	29	30

Waitrose

~~Pancakes that you can warm up~~

Yeo Valley Greek Yoghurt

FLORA

Yeo Valley butter

~~Semi skimmed milk~~ whipped cream

~~tempura prawns x2~~

~~whole milk~~

~~Scala Classic Green Pesto~~

~~Spaghetti~~

~~mushrooms.~~

~~Rude Health Granola x2.~~

~~Green Veg.~~

~~Rosemary~~

~~Bananas~~

Tenderstem Brocolli

~~Poilane Sliced Bread~~

~~White Sliced Bread.~~

~~Unsmoked bacon-~~

~~diet~~ Apple Juice.

Tuna tins x ~~2 or 3~~.

~~Baked Ready Salted Walkers~~ Crisps.

~~Plain cooked chicken-~~

~~Cream Crackers. JACOBS.~~

~~Good Orange Juice.~~

~~Prime fillet~~ salmon

~~Halibut~~

monkfish.

~~soy sauce~~

4. What is the name of the force pulling the skydiver down? - **slide 8-9**

The force is called gravity

5. What is the name of the force trying to push the parachute and skydiver up? - **slide 10 - 11**

air ressistance

6. What forces do you think might be represented by the arrows in this image of the cycle? - **slides 12**

Tea
Toilet roll
kitchen roll
foil
sausages
filo pastry
spinach
observer

Quiche
mushrooms
spinach
cherry toms

fruit / lime / lemon
bananas
aluminium foil
Oat cakes
light olive oil

---

pud?

> chicken
> veg
> face cream / soap
> wine
> fizzy water

snap eggs

- red grapes (big, red
- mash potatoes
- innocent orange ju
- ~~onion & garlic~~
- onion & garlic
- still lemonade

- detol hand
- Broccoli
- can of chickp
- loose sweet p
  x 2 (if no
- jar of tahi

Return Address: PO Box 100081, Nottingham NG2 9LX

IKA ENVC51

THERE ARE A NUMBER of lists in the collection that give me particular pleasure for a variety of reasons. I'm as much drawn to the calligraphic nature of the handwriting as I am to the substance of the list. As someone with experience in the visual arts, it is often this balance between form and content that I find most compelling. I have a particular fondness for redacted lists. These bold graphic gestures, where the shopper emphatically obliterates items as they enter the trolley or basket, have a real sense of immediacy, purpose and achievement. As if, 'There, that's the cereal sorted!'

I am also particularly attracted to those lists where the shopper has approached their task in a regimental and ordered way, with the items arranged topographically. Fruit and veg appear top left; pasta and rice are indicated accurately to reflect the position of the third aisle; cheese and beneath this milk are found around the middle of the list, then household cleaning and personal hygiene next, and finishing off with bread bottom right and wine top right. Waitrose's recent reordering of the goods in many aisles will have been a particular, if temporary, irritation to the topographic list-writer.

One of my favourite lists was found in the car park on a dark, very wet evening. When I lifted the completely sodden, neatly folded sheet of paper from the tarmac, I instantly sensed that it was a rich find. Careful not to tear the delicate sheet, I gently separated the paper at the corners and opened it to its full A4 size. The shopper had used a blue ink pen to write their intended purchases in one long, straight column very close to the full length of the short edge of the paper. It was titled 'Shopping List' with each item neatly preceded by a bullet point. A second, shorter list appears at 90 degrees, emanating from the centre of the sheet and close to the paper crease – apparently written when the sheet had been folded twice. Many of the items repeat those listed in the longer list but were not prefixed by bullet points. The complete saturation from the rain combined with the double folding from A4 to postcard size has caused the ink to permeate through the paper three times. The front shows the original lists, which are then mirrored and reversed before finally appearing ghostly and indiscernible. The back of the list is equally, if not perhaps more, seductive. The palimpsestic potential of the obscured and overlapping texts creates a disintegrated calligraphic abstraction, leaving a balanced and fragile composition just beyond readability.

I wonder if the author of this list would have also enjoyed the simple, serendipitous intervention of the weather's transformational impact.

Shopping List

- honey
- tea
- coconut water
- spinach
- rocket
- watercress
- carrot
- broccoli
- bell pepper
- black olives
- lemon
- lime
- avocado
- olive oil
- onion
- garlic
- celery
- courgette
- vegetable stock
- green beans
- green peas
- asparagus
- pineapple
- cucumber
- apples

Honey
Spinach
Rocket
Carrot
Cucumber
Broccoli
Olives
Lemon
Lime
Avocado
Pineapple juice
Blueberries
Yoghurt
Squash
Washing powder

Strawberries (Spanish cheap)

Grapes

Blueberries

Bananas

Tomatoes small

Cucumber

(yellow if poss.)

Juice, Cole Slaw, Beet Root

Humus, Sausage,

Chicken?

~~[illegible]~~

Pizza

Spaghetti

Oven Chips, Ice Cream

Filters for Coffee

Eggs!

milk!

Cheese

Yoghurt

French Stick

Wholemeal

toast

Cake

Water

Beer

TP

Weleda Calendula Baby Oil, Fragrance free!

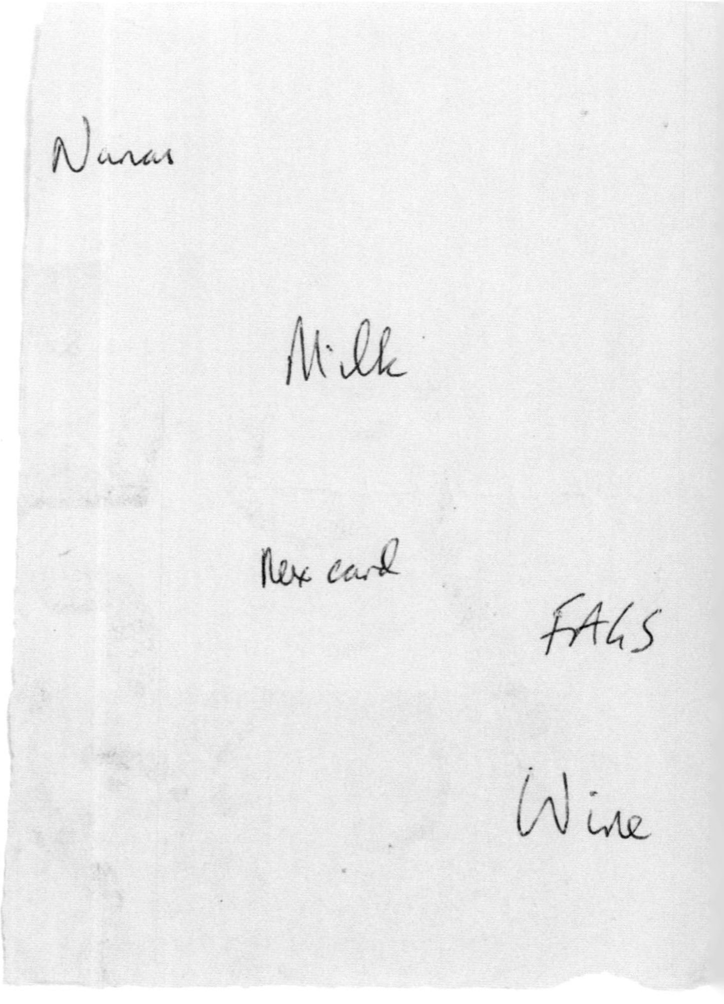
Nanas

Milk

Rex card

FAGS

Wine

Fruit
Veg

Milk
Butter

Tea
Coffee

B. Bars

T Paste

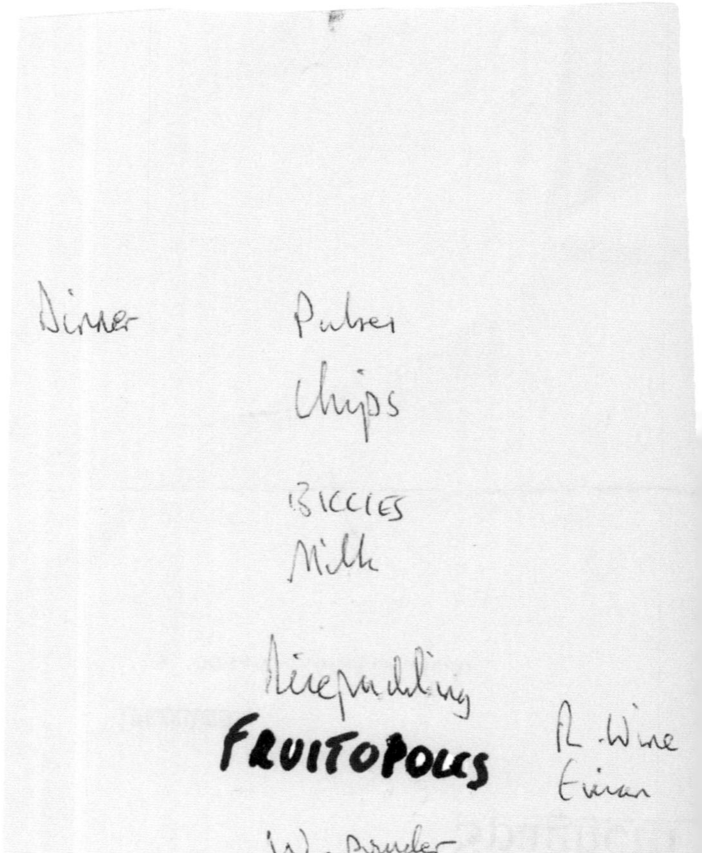

Dinner

Pulses

Chips

BICCIES

Milk

Ricepudding

FRUITOPOLIS

R. Wine

Evian

W. powder

T. Paper

- ☐ goose fat
- ☐ potatoes
- ☐ peas / summergreens
- ☐ ~~mint, parsley + tarragon~~
- ☐ celery?
- ☐ Lemons x 3 + 1 orange.
- ☐ Thyme, Rosemary, Sage.
- ☐

Thyme, 
Rosemary, 
~~Bay~~,
Sage.  fluffy

Collect Anna's present in Waitrose

- 2 x Italian red wine <u>Triade</u>
- orange sorbet
- 2 x Sauvignon blanc wine

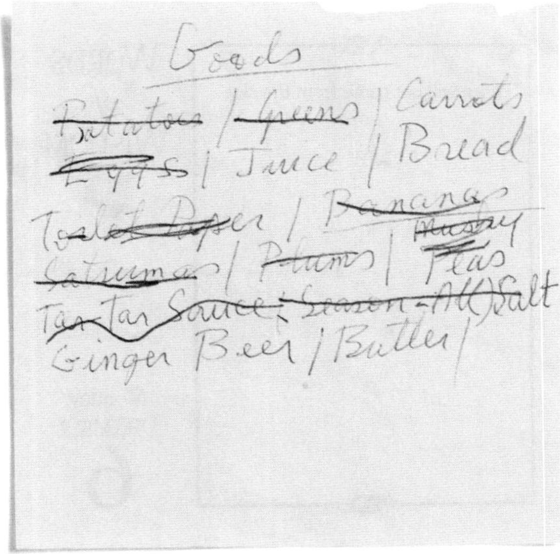

Goods

Potatoes | Greens | Carrots
Eggs | Juice | Bread
Toilet Paper | Bananas
Satsumas | Plums | Mushy Peas
Tar-Tar Sauce | Season-All Salt
Ginger Beer | Butter |

Peace will not come from the sky.

WORDS of WISDOM

Monday
DECEMBER
6

shopping Masking tape

- PESTO ask for a double portion

- Berries · chickpeas
- Bread · red pepper
- Cheese · mandarins
- Carrots · Bananas
- Beans · NUTS
- Broccoli · lentils
- grapes · mushroom
- coffee maker black bin bags
- potatoes 100 roll
- spagghetti
- parsley nappies
- garlic
- coffee coffee
- tortellini (· cheese biscuits
- rice · magazines
- cereal x2
- Peanut Butter
- Marmelade · chocs

· hummus
· pesto
· pasta

wellies
Balls
Ergobabby
Buckets
all weathers

pots + covers white + wine

dried fruits

honey
planters

LEGO
roll of paper
pens
paints
cards
Sticker Book
cards
Reading Books
Sketch Book
TAPE
Boys Adventure Book
Atlas (road + British Isles
piano Book
home learning

F	brocoli; pizzas; carrots
S	cheesghetti spaghetti greenbeans.
S	cheese garlic bread sausages broccoli
M	tortellini pasta carbonara pesto

(pesto)

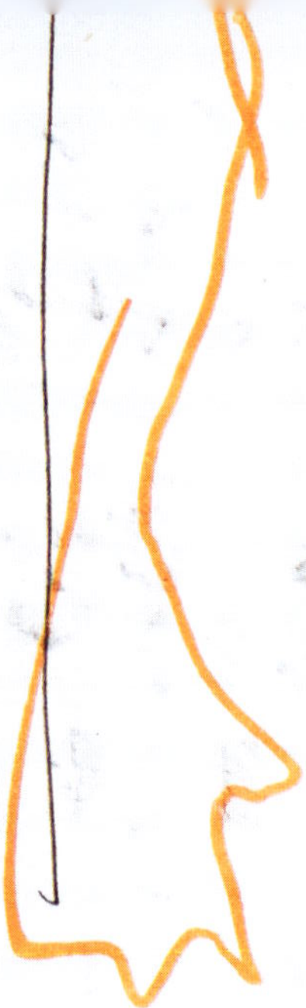

East Somerset Railway
BA4 4QP
Shepton Market

Great Western Railway
Swindon

Stonehenge

SIL		HAMS		CROISANTS	
JEBERRIES		OLIVES			
OCCOLI		PORK PIE			
RROTS		CHEESE			
ILLIES				**DRY FOOD**	
RIANDER		**CHILLED ITEMS**		CANNED FOOD	
NGER		BOLOGNESE SAUCE		BISCUITS	✓
LE		COLESLAW SALAD		CHOCOLATE	
TURCE		FALAFELS		EGGS	
IONS	✓	FRESH PASTA		FLOUR	
RSLEY		HUMUS		MUESLI	
RSNIPS		PANCETTA		PASTA	
ARS		SOUPS			
TATOES				**CAT FOOD**	
SBERRIES				DRY	✓
D PEPPERS		**MEATS**		WET	
NNER BEANS		CHICKEN			
NAGE		BEEF	✓	**BABY MAKSI**	
RING ONIONS		LAMP		FORMULA MILK	
AWBERRIES		PORK		BABY RICE	

		DIARY		TOILETRIES/CLEANING	
NKS		MILK		SOAP	
CE		BUTTER		BLEACH	✓
R	✓	COTTAGE CHEESE		BODY LOTION	
KE		CRAIME FRAICHE		CIF	
MONADE		CREAM		CONDITIONER	
: YOURKSHIRE / HERBAL		PHILADELPHIA		GLASS CLEANER	
TER	✓	YOGHURT		MARBLE CLEANER	
NE				SHAMPOO	✓
				SPONGES	

AKFAST		LUNCH			
ASTED PANINI WITH CHEESE		BOLOGNESE		ROAST CHICKEN	
CON, CHEESE SANDWICH		BEEF STEW		STIR FRY	
F & CUCUMBER SANDWICH	✓	BRODO			
SHROOMS ON TOAST		CHILLI CON CARNE		Ketchup	
NCAKES		COTTAGE PIE			
ACHED EGG & SALMON		CURRY - INDIAN		Cucumbers	
MON BAGEL		CURRY - THAI		Pickled	

Deodorant
toothpaste.
Miso
Toilet roll
Little oats
Milk
Veg
Fruit
Mozarella
Pizza toppings
Tinned items
Cloths

Violoncello.
3
molto espress. e largamente
sonore
espress.
dim.
con sordini
divisi
unis.
Viol. II.

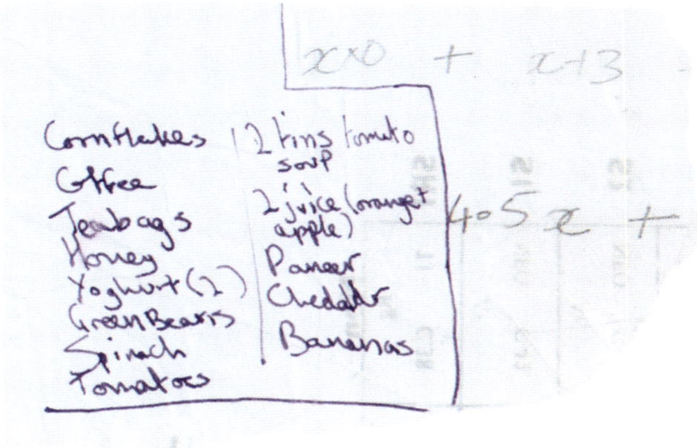

Cornflakes
Coffee
Teabags
Honey
Yoghurt (2)
Green Beans
Spinach
Tomatoes
2 tins tomato soup
2 juice (orange + apple)
Paneer
Cheddar
Bananas
xx0 + x13
405x +

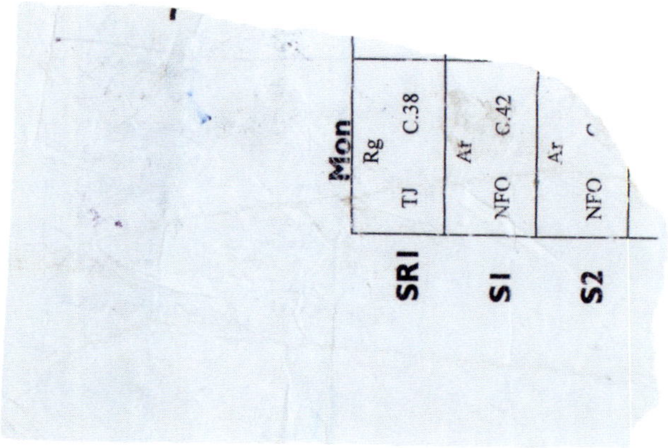

Mon
SR1
TJ
Rg
C.38
S1
NFO
Ar
C.42
S2
NFO
Ar

TUNA
REBRICA
LIMUN
Crumpets
Hot X Buns
Yoghurt
HUMMUS
Artichokes
Prune juice
Apple Struddel
chocolate spread
Peanut butter
dad Birthday
Mustard
Olive oil
Rice
Eggs
Waitrose
Crisps
Coffee
Tonic
Milk
Oyster sauce
Soy sauce
Chicken
MALDON SALT
EGGS
KOMBU
BONITO FLAKES
SUGAR
OATS
BUTTER
OLIVE OIL
Porridge
Patate
Veg.
Toothpaste
Parsley
Chicken

Celery
Chicken
Chicory
figs
beetroot
lime
coriander
ginger
garlic
Soya Milk
Green
Beans
MILK
TOMATOES
NEWSPAPER
Prunes (2)
Avocado (3)
Crunchy Bran
Chillies
Cheese
Berries
Milk (2)
Yogurt (3)
Shreddies
balsamic
tin corn
washing up liq
Ice cream
Cream cleaner
Crunchy Bran
Berries
Shreddies
Parmesan
Yogurts (2)
Loo Roll
Rhubarb Juice
Bread
Matches
Marmalade
Pork loin
Pork Chops
Microwave Veg
apple
salad
cottage cheese
eggs
Toms
Beetroot
veg?
Sausages
chicken OK
napkins
Potatoes
Veg
apple juice
cold meat

Salt
Pibbles
Milk
Cherrios
Bunnies
Burger Buns

THE SHOPPING LIST collector is someone with an innate curiosity for the lives of others. A person who will instinctively construct mental profiles of neighbours they have never spoken to on the basis of observed behaviour, age, dress, hairstyle, exterior of home, etc. This collector is someone who may join the local WhatsApp group, take part in a street party, speak with ease to random people on the street (particularly if they have a dog) or offer directions to anyone looking lost. These actions are usually performed out of a sense of civic spirit, but equally out of basic inquisitiveness.

From a young age, I've had a keen interest in people watching. Kids are good at staring at other people in a completely unselfconscious way, which for adults would be unacceptable. Travelling in the back with my sister on car journeys, I loved peering into other vehicles, particularly when moving slowly or – even better – when a neighbouring car with young passengers had stopped at lights. It was more of a fascination with the whole family unit captured in a glance, than it was an interest in the component individuals. With hindsight, I recognise that what riveted me was the split-second *mise-en-scène* and how it could be interpreted. As I grew older, this curiosity transferred to catching glimpses into people's homes, usually the sitting room, when walking along streets, especially at night. The opportunity to steal a look while travelling by train, as one slows on entering a densely populated cosmopolitan area, hopeful of catching a strangely fleeting domestic scenario, has always tantalised. This was more casual than voyeuristic, more serendipitous and detached. I wasn't setting out to resolve anything about what I saw, but just to take it as fact. These snatched pieces of frozen domestic life had something ordinary but uncannily heroic and dynamic about them.

The urge to capture these incidental, sometimes filmic, moments is also fulfilled in the found shopping list. The transient snapshot image that is gone as soon as it appears is made manifest in the scrap of paper itemising quotidian supermarket purchases. The list provides an opportunity to consider an accumulation of small insights into others' lives and to delve deeper than the fleeting glance permits. The cinematic *mise-en-scène* becomes vignette, and pleasure resides in slow looking.

cotton wool
capers
Garlic
milk
fruit
hummous
Yoghurt
Green Tea
fabric softener ✓
loo ROLL

Bananas

Fs of Forest,

Bread

Milk

Fish Pie

Green Beans

Smoked Cods Roe.

SOS
BIX
MILK
CEREAL
CHEEZ
JAM.
YOG.
BREAD
COCO
IBUP. ROFEN
Nestlé
Shredded Wheat
SINCE 1893

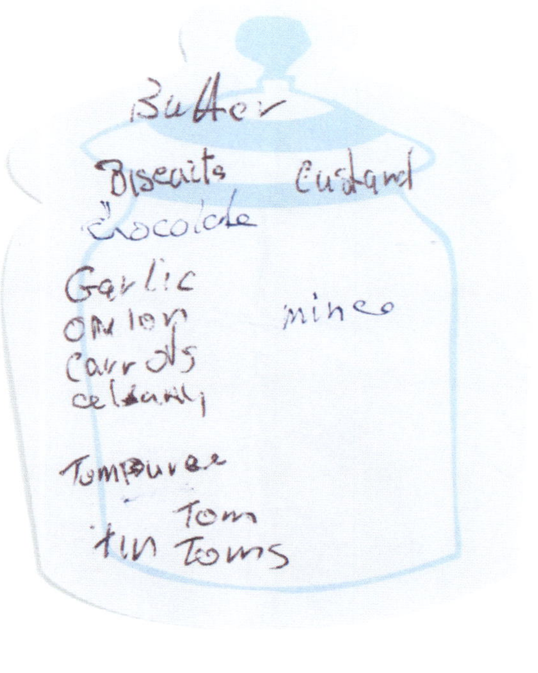
Butter
Biscuits
Custard
Chocolate
Garlic
onion
mince
carrots
celery
Tompuree
Tom
tin Toms

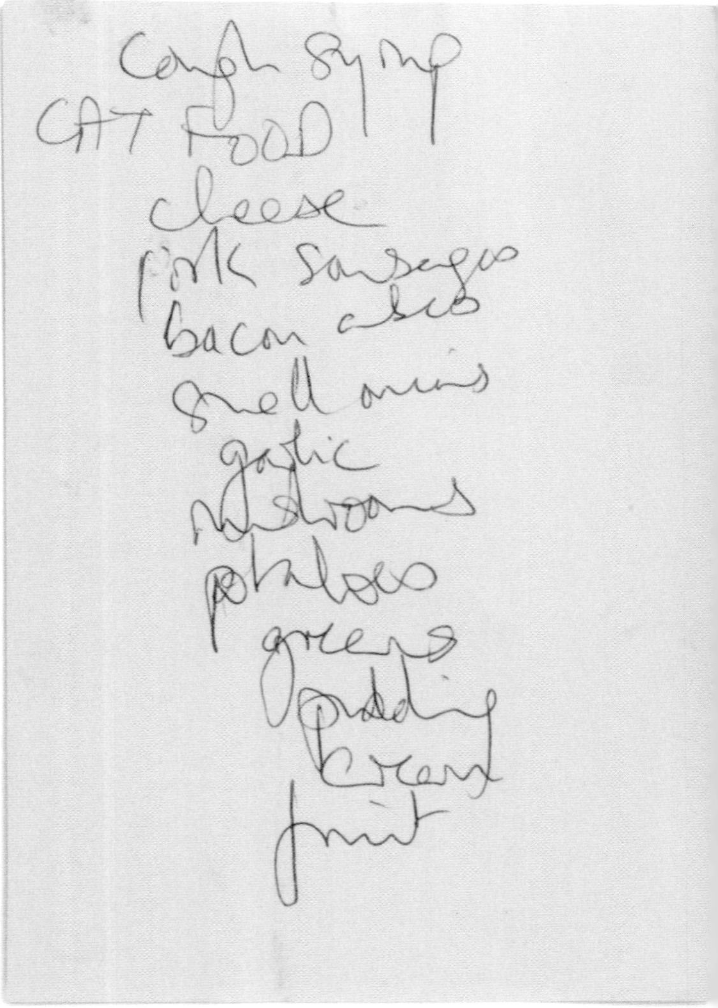
cough syrup
CAT FOOD
cheese
pork sausages
bacon also
small onions
garlic
mushrooms
potatoes
greens
pudding
cream
fruit

from Alexandra Pringle

Dear Lynn,

Hannah's 2nd novel — about the decline & fall of the aristocracy & the bankers. It's pretty delicious.

much love

Alexandra

Editor-in-Chief

Bloomsbury Publishing Plc

50 Bedford Square, London WC1B 3DP +44 (0)20 7631 5847

alexandra.pringle@bloomsbury.com @AlexandraPring www.bloomsbury.com

BLOOMSBURY

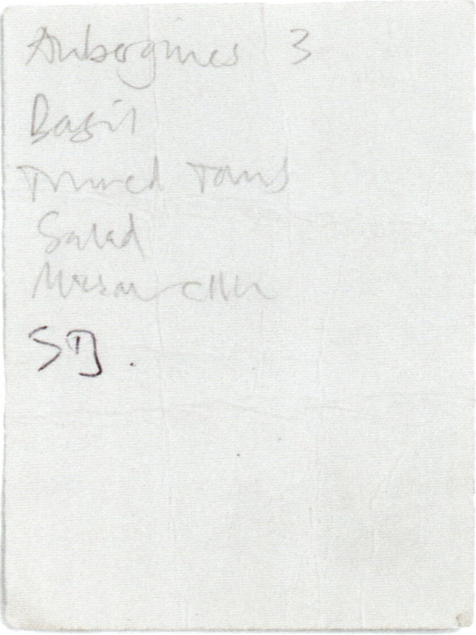
Aubergines 3
Basil
Salad

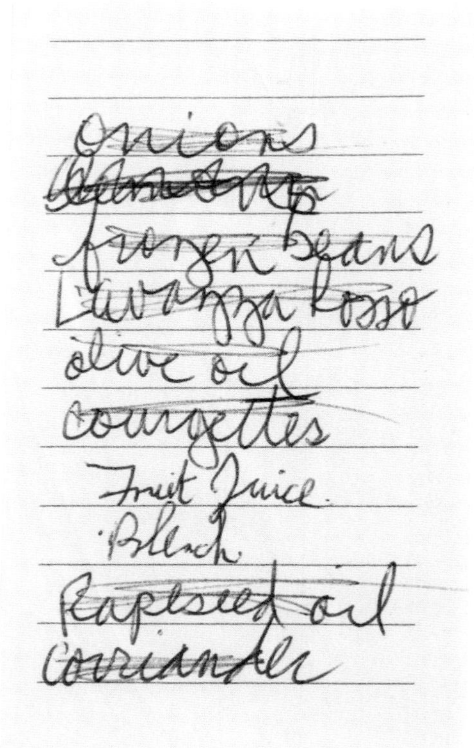
Onions
[illegible]
frozen beans
Lavazza Rosso
olive oil
courgettes
Fruit Juice.
·Bleach
Rapeseed oil
Coriander

baked ?

rasbs, frut. kiwis

eggs,

halou

lentils

tins of beans, small passata,

almonds,

bleach,

make bread,

toilet roll, shampoo.

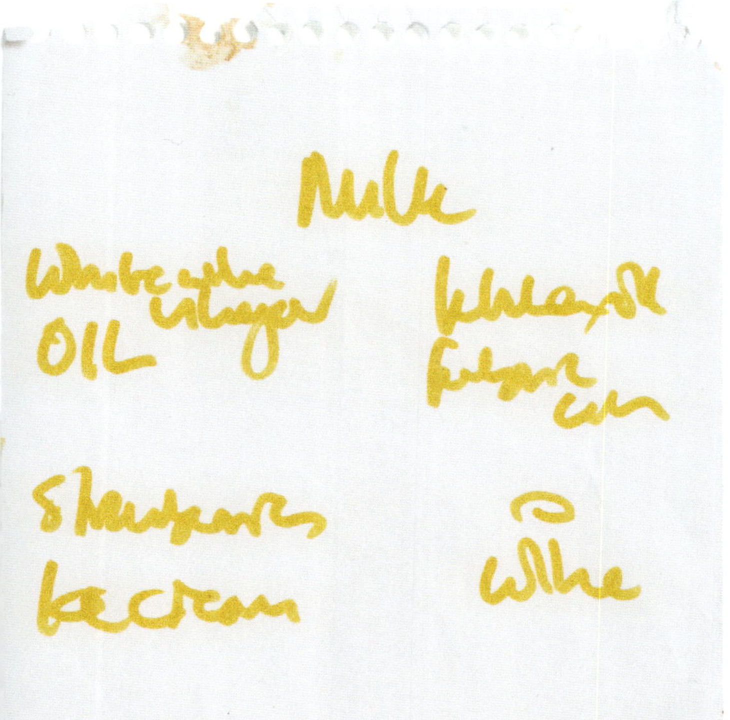
Milk
White wine vinegar
OIL
Strawberries
Ice cream
Wine

fish! milk

cereal Hot Sauc

Soft fruit

Coconut milk

plant food

tin tomatoes

white ~~malt~~ wine vinegar x 6

ran sugar x 10

Cardial

wine

Salt

white mustard seed

Celery seed

Malt vinega

Mushrooms

decaf tea

plaen flaer

biscuits

Soa

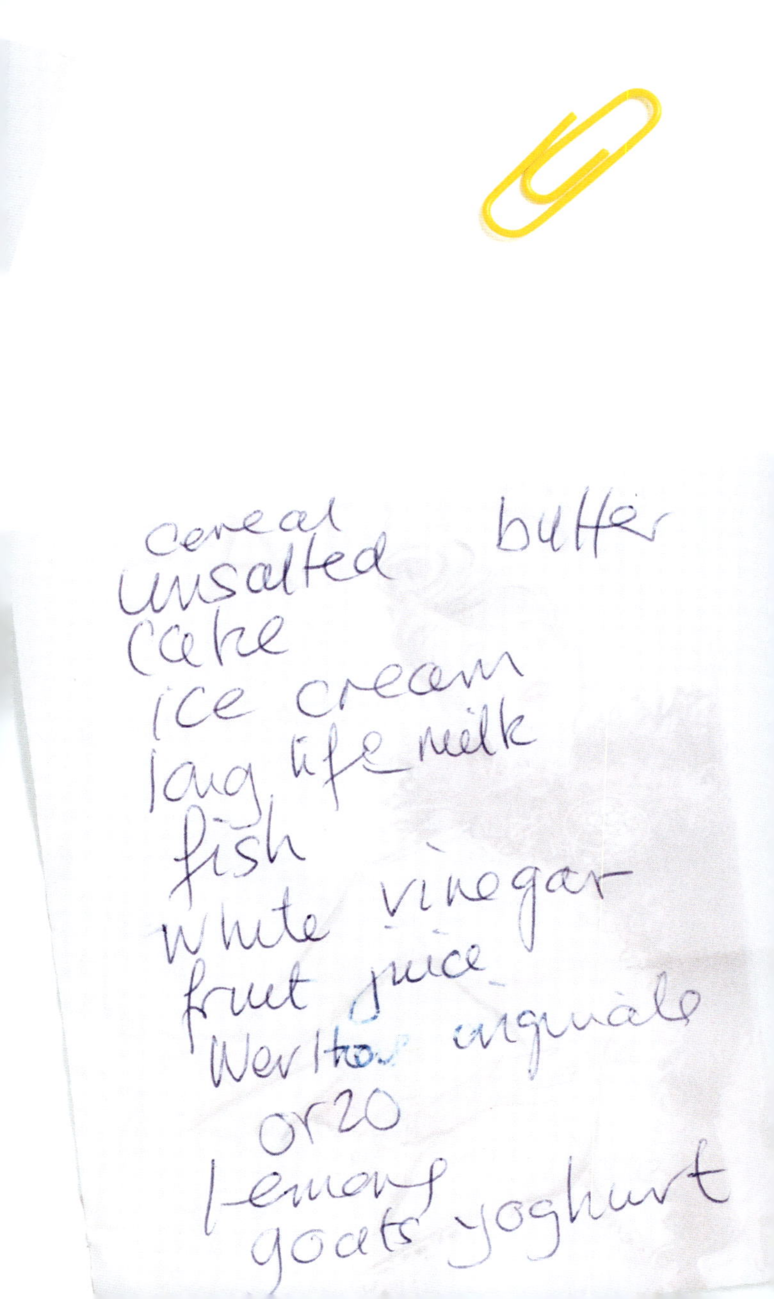
cereal butter
unsalted
cake
ice cream
long life milk
fish
white vinegar
fruit juice
Werthers original
orzo
lemons
goats yoghurt

VANISH SPRAY OUST X2
CLOTHES WASH
?200 ROLLS
ICE
MATZOS
BUTTER X 3
CHEESE
BREAD
SALAD.
SPECIAL K B
KETCHUP.
CRUNCHY NUT
SAT SUPPER / SUN SUPPER
FRUIT
KENYA
DEWAR
ASSAM T.

150g hazelnuts
caster sugar / golden caster
450ml double cream
200 creme fraiche
300g raspberries
Soft fruit

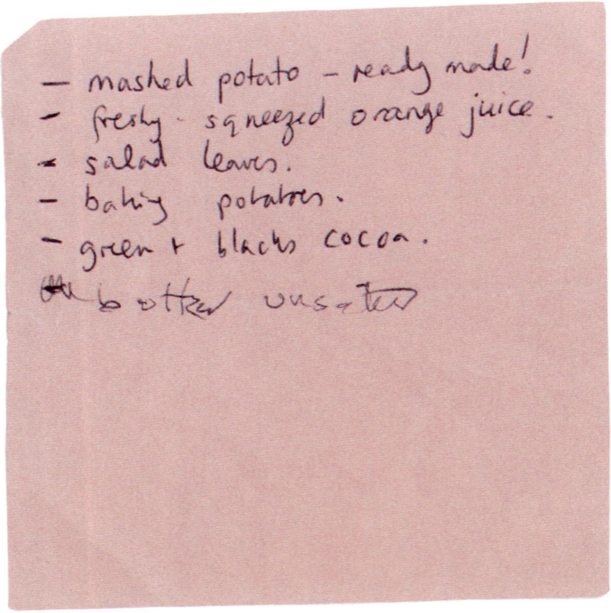

- mashed potato – ready made!
- freshly squeezed orange juice.
- salad leaves.
- baking potatoes.
- green + blacks cocoa.

butter unsalted

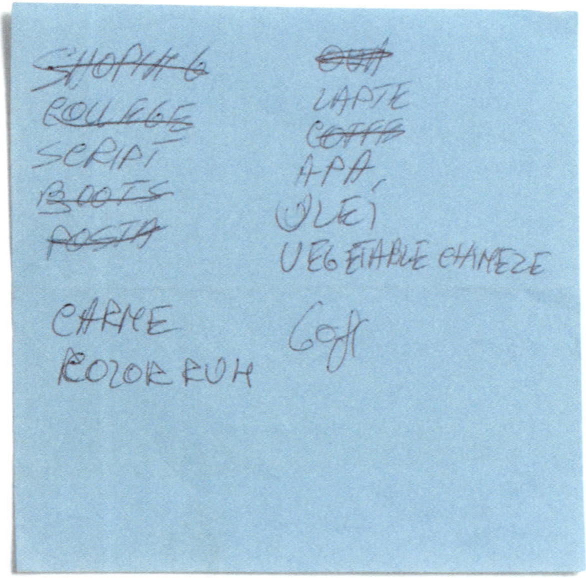

~~SHOPING~~
~~COLLEGE~~
SCRIPT
~~BOOTS~~
~~POSTA~~

CARNE
ROZOKRUH

~~OUA~~
LAPTE
~~COFFE~~
APA
OLEI
VEGETABLE CHANEZE

Goff

kitchen roll
Milk
oranges
bannanas
Chicken
buns spence
burger sauce

More Pasta

Fatigue light

MILK

Tesco stuff

Lidl ?

NUTS

Sweet / Smoked Paprika.

MILK	[illegible] HAND
FROZEN Ps	Wash
CHIPS	CRISPS
ICE	Pilsner
[illegible]	Fizzy G Fruit
Yogurt	[illegible]
	Flowers ?

FISH —

ICE

Fruit + Veg. Potatoes

San Pellegrino · Pompelmo + Fizzy Water

Grapefruit / Orange

Tonics

VEG

Milk Frozen Peas
Chips Ice
Yogurt ~~Gorgonzola~~

Hand Wash | Shower Wash

£20 ~~2 x Crisps. NUTS?~~

~~Pepsi Max~~ ~~Grapefruit Fizz~~
Ginger Beer? ~~Sanpellegrino Water Fizz?~~
Tonics ~~Potatoes.~~
~~Fish?~~

LIST

- Soy Sauce
- Ainsley's chicken & lemongrass soup
- Sellotape
- ~~Brown wrapping paper~~
- Small envelopes
- Loo rolls

Fizzy water

Elder flower

Ciabatta loaf

Frozen Spinach

2 chicken breasts

½ romaine lettuce

Salad leaves

Orange Juice

Red Milk

Beer

Oranges

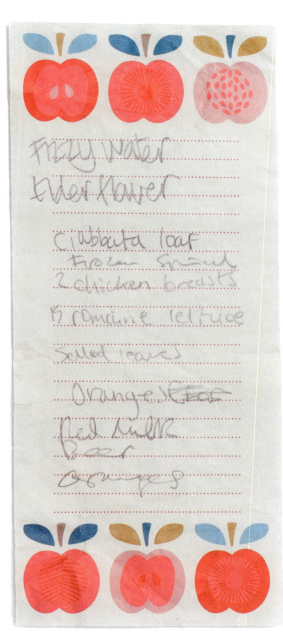

POSTAGE PAID
0050
N3022079
GREAT BRITAIN

LONDON
E2
05 02 15

4 tins beans
4 tins tomatoes
2 tins tuna
Large rice (bags)
kidney beans
pasta sauce (fresh tomato)
tea bags (Yorkshire)
nutella
peanut butter

ribena
orange squash

fresh orange juice
NO apple juice

fruit & fibre
Frosties

onions
mushrooms
celery sticks

cheese biscuits
eggs
pizzas.

potatoes
carrots.

I HAVE NEVER seen a notice that read:

LOST
Shopping List
Black ink on front of DL envelope.
Postmarked 'London E2 05.02.15'.
Listed items include: beans, tuna, tomatoes, rice, kidney beans, celery sticks, etc.
Reward offered – call 020 7555 1234

As yet, it seems that the shopping list has no monetary value.

There are plenty of things that can be found freely (if also at times unlawfully) in nature, which can then be bought or traded commercially, such as seashells, driftwood or pinecones. I had wrongly presumed that beachcombing was similar to shopping list collecting – an unlicensed activity that brought with it the dual pleasure of amassing interesting finds, which you can either keep or discard. So, I shouldn't have been surprised to discover that hag stones (a stone that has a naturally occurring hole in it and is believed to have magical properties) and sea glass (small pieces of glass that have been worn smooth by the sea over decades) are also available for purchase online for just a few pounds via Etsy, eBay and other individual sites. Perhaps I should re-examine my attachment to the bag of hag stones in the cupboard?

The curator Jim Ede (1885–1990) is best known for his art collection that filled Kettle's Yard, his home in the centre of Cambridge, which had been converted from four small cottages in the mid 1950s. But alongside the titans of British and international modernism were domestic items and found objects he'd collected and arranged, and to which he ascribed similar aesthetic value as he did to his art. He is particularly venerated for his *Spiral of Stones* (circa 1958) – a simple and elegant arrangement of 76 hand-gathered spherical pebbles in decreasing sizes placed on a round table under a window. Kettle's Yard is now a museum, and the *Spiral of Stones* remains a favourite exhibit.

On another table nearby, the Scottish poet, artist, writer and gardener Ian Hamilton Finlay (1925–2006) has inscribed onto a smooth, sea-weathered, flat ovoid stone:

KETTLE'S YARD
CAMBRIDGE
ENGLAND IS THE
LOUVRE OF THE
PEBBLE

Value can of course be ascribed to anything and everything, whether material, time or ideas. Supply and demand determines value. As someone who has worked with art throughout their professional life, I have witnessed how a valuation of an artwork can often be misinterpreted as an assessment of its quality or the worth/seriousness of its subject. The two aren't necessarily aligned and the valueless shopping list is proof of this.

Today is 15th

Wine
Beer
Charcutiere
red peppers x 3
onion x 5
celery
garlic
thyme.
puy lentils
Lemon x 5
flat leaf parsley x 3
Watercress/ rocket
200g goats cheese.
onion bahji's
greek yoghurt.
ginger
birds eye chilli's
natural yoghurt.
cardamon pods.
chicken breast.
225g tomatoes

garlic bread
salad
pasta leaves
parmesan
1kg mince
marjoram
butter
milk
okra (150g)
shallots (70g)
loo roll
tomatoes
red onion x 6
Gorgonzola
walnut pieces.
bacon
tom sauce.
breaded chicken
carrots
brocolli.
pizza
cooked chicken.

Nectarines

Non virgin Olive Oil

Olay

Daisy Head

Tonic Cans

Spreadable Butter

Garlic Mayo

[illegible]

[illegible]

Milk

Gin

Chicken

Oyster sauce

Soy sauce

red onion

Ginger

Fruit

Ten Buns.

Beef Stock

Worcestershire Sauce.

Eggs.

185g Dried Pre Soaked Apricots.

125g dessicated coconut.

+ Apricot Jam.

Celery. Crisps.

1½ minced beef / lamb.

NoMad

Kitchen roll
Loo roll
fairy liquid
Clothes wash

bacon
Chicken
mince 800g

carrots
celery
potatoes
ham

Parmesan
cheddar
Milk
butter
brown bread
Non cook lasagne
p
ice
Coleslaw

chips
Chopped tomatoes
Soda water

Shopping List

Toothpaste
Milk
Water
Bread

Nominays
TCSC
Sam re gambre
Lizzie / Rob
Richard
Clare Hopkinson
Manon re Wales gol Phyllis
Richard Morgan re Polo

info@magpieanting.co.uk

Quiche mui Henrietta
Biomass Bw
Shoalumi
Andreia
Jamil Stephanie Summer
Cheesy biscuits Lexi
S Bedman N-J
Rawhide/pulp Celia
Anthony

- עוף שלם
- טחון בקר וכבש ?
  2 של אחד
- חזה שניצלים
- חומוסים
- עגבניות
- חסה
- פלפלים
- פירות: מנגו
  תפוחים ירוקים
  בננה
- אורז בסמטי
- מקרונים בקופסה
- סלמון - טרי
- Creme fraiche
- יוגורטים לבנים 3%

- עלי רוזמרין
- חלב x 3
- 3 x feta
- just roll puff pastry x3
  ירוק
- מוצום

Shop

- ~~Beurre 2×2~~
- ~~[illegible] Garlic~~
- ~~oignons~~ ~~Hog sticks~~
- ~~Papier cadeau~~
- ~~tortillas~~ + ~~beef steak haché~~
- ~~viande hachée~~ - ~~poulet~~
- ~~carottes~~ ~~choux~~ ~~oignons~~
- ~~[illegible]~~
- ~~tomates pelées~~ ~~Yaourt~~
- ~~[illegible]~~
- gingembre + pamplemousse
- ~~bagel~~ - ~~pâtes~~
- ~~[illegible]~~
- ~~mangue~~ - ~~chou vert~~
- ~~double crème~~ - ~~vanille~~
- ~~Biscuits~~
- ~~poulet (fajitas)~~
- ~~apéro~~
- ~~orgeat~~
- lingettes
- cartouches?

- ~~PQ~~
- ~~Sopalin~~
- ~~Confiture~~
- Eau
- ~~fromage~~
- ~~saumon~~
- ~~fumé~~
- Pain
- ~~fish fingers (kinder ...)~~
- ~~2 pâtes feuilletées congelées~~

Printed on 100% Recycled Paper

Lentils
Water bread
Juices / Yogourt
onions
vegetables stock
Cerial
pears
blue berries
fish / or mussels
chicken breast
oysters
lemons
White wine

BEEF BURGERS

GRANNIE SMITH'S

ROLLS

HAM.

DINNER SUN..

Dear B and G,

I thought I'd let you know I took it upon myself to feed LPC her blob @ 18:0[illegible] precisely as she was most in need. Thanks for all your kindnesses and nicenesses.

G, have a wonderful fortnight in the wordless wild.

B, see you soon no doubt!

X Luke

P.S. The neo-brinjal has been left for a later day as my aching bones and heavy bag needed a much help a[illegible] poss.

- Rolled oats
- Sunflower oil
- strong wholemeal flour
  " white
- sesame seeds

* Bananas
fresh veg etc---

3 Veg; carrots lettuce, ~~6~~ 5 potatoes

Packet ham Spaghetti, pepp

1 chicken, fish, meat

olives, Pickles,

frozen ~~peas~~,

Greek cheese, butter,

Yogurt,

Coke

Kleenex

weet pot.
Pineapple

meat pot, 2 sweet pot
lettuce carrots [illegible] pie, figs
salami,
meat fish
biscuits
stilton
bin liners
yoghurt
cake

鹽、鸡蛋、蘋果、柑仔、

蝦、豬肉、魚、麵包、

牛油果、朱佐油、

提子、牛油、

POTS
VEG, TOMS,
FRUIT.
HOT DOGS.
EGGS.
PAPERS
WATER
LEMONADE
BRANDY,
M VTS

MAGAZINE,
TRIFLE

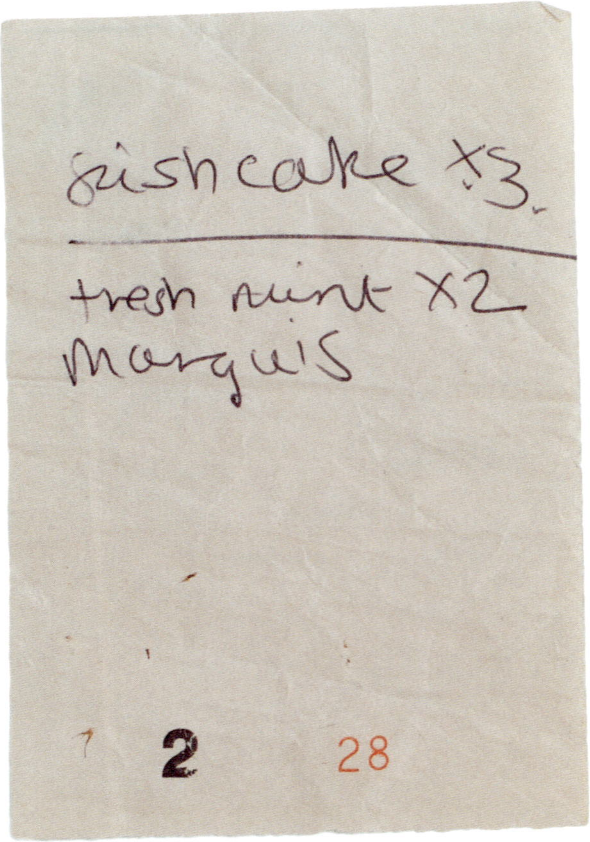

fish cake x3

fresh mint x2
marquis

2 28

SAT

shortcrust pastry
chicken breasts
leeks (3)
creme fraiche (300ml/10floz)

lettuce
cucumber
cress

SUN

Lamb chops
new potatoes
cabbage
cauliflower
mushrooms

MON

chicken
apples
cream
mushrooms
potatoes
pork
peas

T

ga

M

ba

Ti

Thurs (2)

~~chicken~~
~~red pepper~~
~~mushroom~~
~~cream~~
~~rice~~

Fri

~~gammon steaks~~
~~baking potatoes~~
~~mushrooms~~
~~4 tomatoes~~
~~lemon~~ (1)
~~onion~~

THURS 3/10 FROM 335

x 2 BREAD

? 1 MILK

4 DINNERS ? 3 + 1

1 JAM

ORANGES

C1 PUD

TOM + CHEESE

P/SALAMI ?

› 1 PAPER

PICKLED
S. ONIONS

?

Frozen peas

(B) (1) Toothpaste

Ready brew (Red)

Salad veg

cigs / cleansing wipes

Crackers (ord)

lettuce / milk

~~Pears~~ / apples

Toilet paper

Washing powder

vitamins

gaviscon

cash | cigs

marmite

crackers | Kotwo

~~Flash~~ |

Toms | Beetroot

milk x 2

Kitchen towels

apples | Flash bath

cakes

toilet paper

nurofen

| Small ready brek

Rikoda | gaviscon

bananas

LIST COLLECTING CONTINUED apace until the beginning of 2022 but has since tailed off significantly. It is no accident that the easing of the collecting coincided with my decision to leave my job of 23 years to work in a freelance capacity. The practical explanation for the sudden reduction in numbers of lists collected is that there were fewer opportunities, simply because my daily bike commute ended. Greatly reduced visits to Waitrose = greatly reduced lists found.

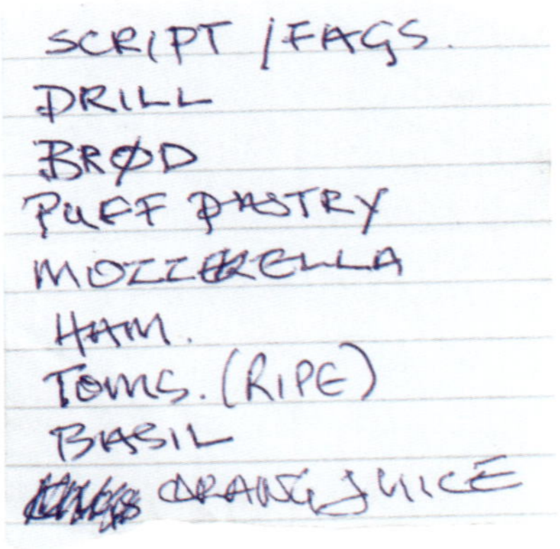
SCRIPT / FAGS.
DRILL
BRØD
PUFF PASTRY
MOZZERELLA
HAM.
TOMS. (RIPE)
BASIL

Major disruption to one's daily rhythm can cause acute stress. Economic considerations aside, the anxiety that accompanied the impending professional gear-change was seismic. At the time, I had not contemplated the additional impact of jettisoning two character-defining rituals in my life – cycling and list collecting. With the benefit of some critical and emotional perspective one year on and counting, it is evident that the shopping list has continued to be a potent source of engagement.

Dish Washer Salt, (Rinse Softener)
Batteries, Carots, Parsnips, Potatoes
Tea, Sugar, Eggs, Beans Biscuits
Soups in Tins, Milk, Bread, Cheese
oxo's. Leg of Lamb, Ham, Cornbeef.
21st B/card, (Bottles Water) Brocco Sauce
Spargetti

~~toilet freshner aqua~~

~~Aquafresh toothpaste x 2~~

~~silver~~

Lavazza ground coffee x 2

lettuce

Kipper

milk x 4 pints

grapes but only good

clementines

tomatoes cucumbers

~~1 courgettes~~

blueberries

~~1 big aubergine~~

1 sweet potato

~~3 red peppers~~

1 packet green beans

bread

avocado

~~Boots bags~~

~~Sudafed nose drops~~

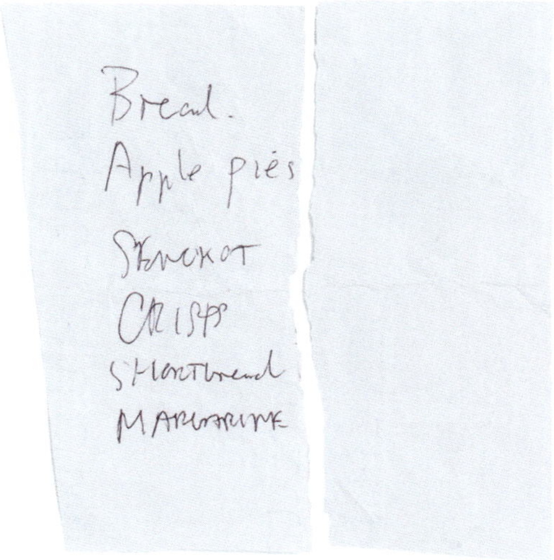
Bread.
Apple pies
CRISPS
Shortbread
MARGARINE

Tanti Augu
Remo
Daniela
Famili
Cappella
x x x x

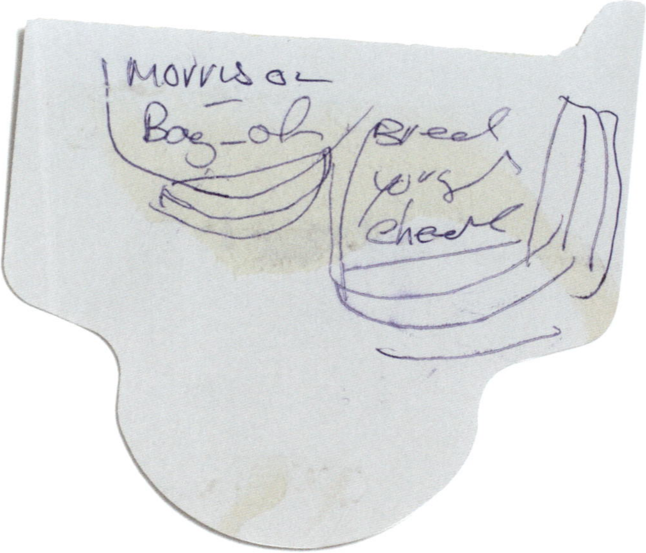
Morrisons
Bag - oh
Bread
yog
cheese

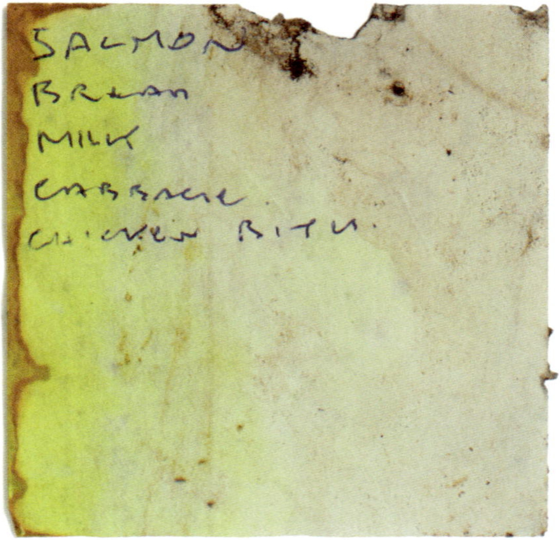
SALMON
BREAD
MILK
CABBAGE
CHICKEN BITS.

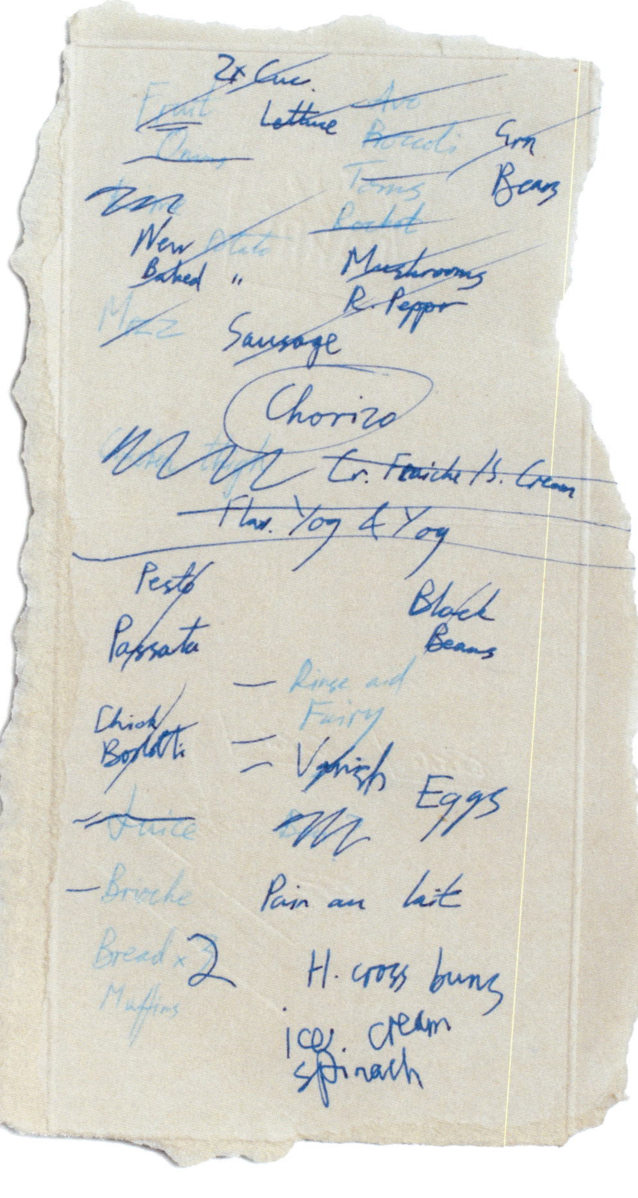
2x Cuc.
Fruit
Lettuce
Avo
Onions
Broccoli
Grn Beans
Toms
Rocket
New Potato
Baked "
Mushrooms
R. Pepper
Mozz
Sausage
Chorizo
Cr. Fraiche H. Cream
Flav. Yog & Yog
Pesto
Black Beans
Passata
— Rinse aid
Fairy
Chick
Borlotti
— Spinach
Eggs
Juice
— Brioche
Pain au lait
Bread x 2
Muffins
H. cross buns
ice cream
spinach

Shopping list

Eggs, bread, cereal, milk, juice, jam, squash,
berocca, bananas, blueberries, yoghurt
Cocoa, eggs, SR flour, butter, ~~cake~~
sugar, 150g choc, double cream, apricot
1.5 kg topside. 2x onions. 2x carrots.
celery. bulb garlic, thyme & rosemary
balsamic + rice wine vinegar
potatoes. peas
Soup.
bacon
Red pepper. chorizo. tinned toms. X2
Onion. Mushrooms. Carrots

Street, Manchester M60 0AL.

10/09 UT.59

Libry
Kitch Roll
Apples
cabbag ?
green smoothie
ginger syrup
tamarind

---

oranges
Ginger syrup
Yogurt
~~Kiwi~~
Tim Tams

...es (ground)
fruit
...gar)

~~paste~~
~~...ssues~~
~~...el sauce~~
~~digestive~~

~~Fed Cake~~
~~397g Can...~~
450g alu...
225g Cas...
5 eggs

INGRID SWENSON is a curator and writer. She has curated exhibitions for a number of contemporary arts institutions in London and elsewhere including the ICA, Whitechapel Gallery, Serpentine Galleries, the Contemporary Art Society, and recently Turner Contemporary. From 1998 to 2021 she was the director of acclaimed arts organisation, PEER, whose ethos is to present the highest quality art as part of everyday life. At PEER, she commissioned projects with over 150 UK-based and international artists including Martin Creed, Mike Nelson, Siobhán Hapaska, Fiona Banner, Danh Võ, Jadé Fadojutimi, Samson Kambalu and Lubna Chowdhary. She was awarded an MBE in 2018 for services to arts in East London. She is passionate about communicating visual art's ability to connect people and ideas across cultures, generations, and geographies.